Breaking Into Information Security: Learning the Ropes 101

Teaching You The Core Fundamentals For Getting Your Career Started in Penetration Testing.

Andy Gill

Breaking into Information Security: Learning the Ropes 101

Teaching You The Core Fundamentals For Getting Your Career Started in Penetration Testing.

Andy Gill

ISBN 9781549903588

© 2016 - 2022 Andy Gill

Also By Andy Gill

Expanding Your Security Horizons: Learning The Ropes 102

Thanks to the Community, for the sharing, the knowledge and the feedback :-)

Onwards to greater things folks!

If this is a physical copy, you've got one of the limited runs, I might even sign it!

Contents

1. Introduction 1
   What this Book is 1
   Why Does This Book Exist? 2
   Who Is This Book for? 3
   A Word of Warning 4
   Disclaimer 4
   Prerequisites 5
   About The Author 6

2. Core Fundamentals 9
   Numbers in Security 9
   Fundamental Networking 11
   Facilitating Attacks with DNS 18

3. Operating Systems 23
   Linux 23
   Windows 26
   MacOS 33

4. Virtualisation 35
   What is Virtualisation? 35
   What it is Used For 35
   Setting Up Your First Virtual Machine 36
   Other Platforms 37

Follow me on Twitter https://twitter.com/ZephrFish

CONTENTS

5. Programming **39**
    Logic 39
    The Basics - Functions, Variables, Learning 42
    Language Types 44

6. Infrastructure **49**
    Reconnaissance 50
    Scanning 59
    Exploitation 80
    Pivoting/Further Recon/Post-Exploitation 82
    Other Types of Infrastructure Testing 88

7. Web Application Testing **101**
    Introduction 101
    Tooling 102
    Methodologies 116
    Note Taking and Session Tracking 125

8. Importance of Reporting **133**
    Reporting in Pentesting 134
    Making Things Beautiful 137
    Technical Findings 137
    Bug Bounty Reporting 143

9. Social & People Skills **149**
    Meetups 150
    Conferences 151

10. Penetration Testing, Bug Bounty Hunting &
    <Insert Colour Teaming> **153**
    Penetration Testing 154
    Bug Bounty Hunting 155
    Coloured Teams 156

11. Hacking Your Career Path 163
    Things to Consider 163
    Advertising Skillset 164
    Selling Yourself 165

12. Further Reading & Resources 173
    Books to Read 173
    Network Pentesting 173
    Programming 174
    Web Application Testing 174
    Quick Reference for Bag 175
    Web Applications for Learning on 176
    People to Follow on Twitter 177
    Links to Checkout 178
    Thank You 179

Follow me on Twitter https://twitter.com/ZephrFish

1. Introduction

Thanks for downloading or picking up a copy of this book whether you spent a few quid or downloaded a free copy(or pirated it as some folks feel the need!), I hope you enjoy it. The version you are reading has been through several revisions; however, the original was about a year in the making. I continue to write blog posts on a bi-monthly basis to expand on specific topics and pick up new ones. The book is aimed primarily at those interested in breaking into the information security industry with a focus on offensive security.

It is also suitable for anyone who has even the faintest interest in information technology/security. The main theory behind it being, that it should serve as an aid for newbies looking for resources and information on security & hacking. It does not contain the be-all and end-all of knowledge; you will need to do some googling for some concepts if you want to learn more.

What this Book is

The book itself is a combination of post on topics from my Blog[1] & other additional topics to get your feet wet. The fact that you're this far says you have taken the time to download and open the eBook or are lucky enough to have a physical copy! In 2020 I made the book permanently free so, if you

---

[1] https://blog.zsec.uk

Follow me on Twitter https://twitter.com/ZephrFish

have taken the time to purchase the ebook or a print copy, thank you! Any funds from the book profits get fed back into the upkeep of my Blog and infrastructure.

The core topics are available for free on my Blog under Learning the Ropes 101[2] series if you can't afford a few quid. However, some topics are not on my Blog and exist solely within this book for your reading pleasure. If you have any requests for topics you'd like to see more of, please message me on Twitter, and I'll happily help.

I have a mini-plan, and I want to keep this up to date as the years and times progress; this might mean updates being pushed out for readers on new topics when they are required if the subject is big enough, I will write a chapter however most of the time it will become a blog post. To keep up to date with all the things I post, I recommend checking out my Twitter[3] & Blog[4].

Why Does This Book Exist?

I started writing a blog in early 2014 to upload write-ups, projects and other tips. One of my good friends (fuzz_sh[5] came to me in 2015 asking me to explain specific topics and expand more on how to follow the path of security so I obliged and wrote the learning the ropes 101 series as an aid for him. Given my working background in security and IT, I found it more beneficial to upload posts about things I had been working on. For two reasons, mainly, the first was for my Blog to serve as an online repository of personal notes that

---

[2] https://blog.zsec.uk/tag/ltr101/
[3] https://twitter.com/ZephrFish
[4] https://blog.zsec.uk
[5] https://twitter.com/fuzz_sh

I could refer back to at any point (how selfish of me!). This became a helping hand for others which is the second reason I continue to write posts. I believe the best form of learning is that if you can explain a topic to a wide range of others, you will learn more about it, yourself.

This book exists because it was suggested and requested by several of my followers on Twitter[6], who voiced a suggestion of making an on-the-go resource for beginners to refer to. It also happens because of a fellow hacker, friend and author who inspired me to write more; Peter Yaworski[7]. He has written a great eBook[8] about web hacking 101, which holds a collection of bug bounty reports and tips. His book is solely based upon bug bounty reports and findings within different programs; however, it is interesting. I would recommend you check it out if bug bounties are something you'd like to get into.

Who Is This Book for?

It is aimed primarily at folks who are starting out wanting to specialise in information security(also referred to as InfoSec). If you've even looked at fundamental IT/development, you may find some of this interesting to read. It is mainly written for the individual looking to get into offensive security(Penetration Testing) but not sure where to start or what to read first.

What this book does do though, is assume a level of technical knowledge and fundamental understanding of bits and pieces,

---
[6]https://twitter.com/ZephrFish
[7]https://twitter.com/yaworsk
[8]https://leanpub.com/web-hacking-101

however, should you not understand something, the easiest way to learn is to search it up on the Internet. Some of us learn by doing and others learn by reading.

A Word of Warning

Warning: This book may contain nuts...

Seriously though, this book is purely my opinion on topics required to give you a solid footing to break your way into the information security industry.

Before diving into the super technical bits and bobs, it is vital for anyone who wants to learn the ropes to understand it is all on **you**. It is up to you to self-learn/self-teach, if you lack the motivation to learn, you're not going to get far in the security sector.

This book will not guarantee land you a job in InfoSec, nor will it give you magic powers or make you a millionaire or immortal...

What it will do, though, is give you a better understanding of some basics and hopefully prepare you a bit more for the real world!

Disclaimer

All the information in this book is published for general information purpose only. Any misuse of the information provided by LTR101 is strictly at your own risk.

I am not responsible for any content on links provided throughout. I have aimed to deliver only ethical links, but sites can change their content at any time. If you find an inappropriate link, please let me know, and I will remove it.

IN SHORT- "HACKING IS ILLEGAL" please use common sense. The difference between hacking and ethical hacking/penetration testing usually boils down to "permission" do not try things on systems, networks, and sites that you do not have expressed written permission to test on or you own them. Permission from a site or organisation on a bug bounty platform comes in the form of the scope; if you shy away from this, you can get yourself in trouble.

Prerequisites

There are no actual requirements to start reading this book except possibly reading (you could get someone to read it to you, though, so that isn't a game stopper). Some examples will require you to have a computer to run things on; you may already be there so not to worry! If not, it's not a core requirement but can help you understand things to a fuller extent. Additionally, if you are reading this in physical form, there are a lot of URLs and links throughout; feel free to pick up the eBook as it is free (as of 2020!).

Additional pre-requisites would be how to use google[9] and some fundamental understanding of maths arithmetic/binary. There are sections in this book that explain basic binary and maths for networking. However, if this topic matter interests you, I suggest looking up google for more information.

---
[9] http://lmgtfy.com/?iie=1&q=how+do+I+use+google+to+search+things%3F

About The Author

I am a hacker at heart, a penetration tester (pentester) who's always been interested in taking things apart and sometimes even putting them together again (in fact, I spent a good few years in computer repair and data recovery). As my day job, I am a security consultant through and through, with a passion for offensive security; I specialise in red teaming and simulated attacks. With a hunger for knowledge and paying it forward, I actively help grow the community by mentoring and educating the masses on security awareness basics.

At the time of writing, I have been in the IT security industry for just over ten years; over these ten years, he has worn many hats in the offensive and defensive/collaborative sphere.

To back up my years in industry, I also hold several other certifications and accolades, including OSCP, OSWP, CCT & A few others[10].

Coupled with my day job, I also participate in bug bounty programs, having reported bugs to over a hundred vendors, including high profile targets such as the US Dept. of Defense, NVIDIA, MindGeek, Facebook and Oracle.

For those that don't know me, I am a strong believer in passing knowledge on and supporting the infosec community I (attempt to) do this by providing tutorials on my Blog (Blog.zsec.uk), running my local DEF CON Chapter[11] & I have also published a book (the one you're reading right now!). Equally, I also volunteer at DEF CON[12] as a SOC Goon (Red

---

[10]https://blog.zsec.uk/offsec-achievements-unlocked/
[11]https://twitter.com/dc44141
[12]https://www.defcon.org/

Follow me on Twitter https://twitter.com/ZephrFish

Shirt) too, each year (since DC25), assisting the SOC with operations and people flow.

Aside from the Blog and book, I have also started a podcast[13] with one of my good friends learning the ropes much like you, the reader is. For more information, check out his about page[14].

Anyway enough about me, onwards with the learning. Enjoy!

---
[13] https://blog.zsec.uk/dave-andys-weegiecast/
[14] https://blog.zsec.uk

2. Core Fundamentals

Regarding the technological skill-set required in this sector (information security & penetration testing), dialling it down to complete basics is where to start. It is essential to understand and get your head around a few core fundamental topics before proceeding; these include binary/decimal conversion, a little maths, basic networking & basic logic. Armed with these, you will have a firm footing in starting.

The core fundamentals section aims to prepare you with the basics required to move through to other later areas; it also will give you a better understanding of what you are looking at. Some of you may find the maths section boring and ask why it is needed; however, bear with me on this one it'll pay off to understand and hopefully give you a better insight into why it is important.

Numbers in Security

Anyone who has ever looked at networking or IP (Internet Protocol) addresses will have noticed many numbers involved. Some of you may not know what this means.

Firstly, an IP address (for those more technically inclined, I will refer to IPv4[15] as IP addresses for this book) usually will look something like this 1.2.3.4. What does that mean? Can

---
[15] http://www.ciscopress.com/articles/article.asp?p=348253&seqNum=7

I not have an IP of 999.1224.213434.12891? Nope unfortunately not for you, mainly because each section of an IP, also known as an octet, is limited to just 256 different numbers (0-255), which means that IP addresses are limited 0.0.0.0 to 255.255.255.255. This can be taken that the theoretical maximum number of total IP addresses is 4,294,967,296 ($2\wedge32$) however, in practice, this is slightly less.

Ports

Another term that will pop up in conversation a lot is ports; there are a total of 65536 (0-65535) ports in networking and technology. Think of these like running services on a machine or a real-world example, thinking of them as entry points into a building. Imagine a massive structure with 65536 windows and doors, each with a number from 0-65535 painted on.

If I want to get in, I have 65536 options of entry however, if the building owner has any mind for security or common sense, a lot of them will be locked therefore reducing my entry down to just a few.

From a technical standpoint, this is the same on servers; for example, if a server has five (5) ports open: 21, 22, 80, 443, 3389, it has five (5) services running that a user or other service can interact with. These five services can be used to access the server (in order of appearance) over FTP(File Transfer Protocol), SSH(Secure Shell), HTTP(Hypertext Transfer Protocol), HTTPS(Hypertext Transfer Protocol Secure) and RDP(Remote Desktop Protocol).

Fundamental Networking

How Does the Internet Work?

This section will explain how the basics of the internet work at a high level. It will also touch on what is required to browse a website, the process involved and the underlying technology.

TCP/IP & DNS

TCP/IP stands for Transmission Control Protocol/Internet Protocol. It's the Internet's fundamental "control system", and it's two systems in one. In the computer world, a "protocol" is simply a standard way of doing things—a tried and trusted method that everybody follows to ensure things get done correctly. So what do TCP and IP do?

Internet Protocol (IP) is simply the Internet's addressing system. All the machines on the Internet, yours, mine, and everyone else's, are identified by an Internet Protocol (IP) address that takes the form of a series of digits separated by dots or colons. If all the machines have numeric addresses, every device knows exactly how (and where) to contact every other machine.

We usually refer to them by easy-to-remember names (like https://blog.zsec.uk) rather than their actual IP addresses. A relatively simple system called DNS (Domain Name System) enables a computer to look up the IP address for any given website. In the original version of IP, known as IPv4, addresses consisted of four groups of digits, such as 12.34.56.78 or 123.255.212.55, but the rapid growth in Internet use meant that we used up all possible addresses by January 2011.

This prompted introducing a "new" IP system with more addresses, which is known as IPv6, where each address is much longer and looks something like this:

```
1  123a:b716:7291:0da2:912c:0321:0ffe:1da2
```

However, IPv6 has been around for a while; it's still not fully integrated as normality, many businesses have it setup for sites, but it is not as mainstream as IPv4.

The other part of the control system, Transmission Control Protocol (TCP), sorts out how packets of data move back and forth between one computer (in other words, one IP address) and another. It's TCP that figures out how to get the data from the source to the destination, arranging for it to be broken into packets, transmitted, resent if they get lost, and reassembled into the correct order at the other end.

TCP 3-Way Handshake

To fully understand the basics, another topic of the way things work is the 3-Way handshake; in this example, we'll talk about a PC connecting to a server/website over HTTP.

To establish a connection, each device must send a *SYN* packet and receive an *ACK* from the other device, following this; one of the SYNs and one of the ACKs are sent together by setting both of the relevant bits (a message sometimes called a *SYN+ACK*). This makes a total of three messages, and for this reason, the connection procedure is called a three-way handshake.

Subnets

You may have heard the term subnet before when looking into the topic of networking or it might be entirely new for you. Either way, this section will explain what they are why they're essential to know about.

What is a subnet?

A subnetwork or more commonly referred to as subnet, is a section of a greater network. It can represent all the machines at one geographic location, in one building, or on the same local area network (LAN).

...but why?

Having an organisation's network divided into subnets allows for better network segregation and more efficient traffic flow. To quote Cloudflare "Through subnetting, network traffic can travel a shorter distance without passing through unnecessary routers to reach its destination."

What is DNS?

The Domain Name System{s}(DNS) is essentially a phonebook of the Internet. To access information and websites online, this is achieved via the use of domain names, like zsec.uk. Web browsers(Browsers) interact with Internet Protocol (IP) addresses. The service translates human-readable domain names into computer-readable IP addresses to enable browsers to load resources on the Internet.

Every device connected to the Internet will have a unique IP address that other machines use to find the device. DNS servers eliminate the need for humans to memorise IP addresses such as 10.10.200.1 (in IPv4), or more complex newer alphanumeric IP addresses such as FE80::0202:B3FF:FE1E:8329 (in IPv6).

How Does It Work?

DNS as described above basically translates domain names into IP addresses, a DNS lookup(i.e how you browse to a site), can be split up into a series of steps;

1. A user types' zsec.uk' into their web browser, and the request travels into the Internet and is received by a DNS recursive resolver.
2. The resolver then queries a DNS root nameserver(explained below) (.).
3. The root server then takes the request and responds to the resolver with the address of a Top-Level Domain (TLD) DNS server (such as .com, .uk or etc), which stores the information for the domains belonging to that TLD(i.e any .uk domain for the .uk TLD DNS Server). When searching for zsec.uk, our request is pointed toward the .uk TLD.
4. The resolver then requests the .uk TLD server. Which then responds with the IP address of the domain's name server, zsec.uk.
5. Lastly, the recursive resolver sends a query to the domain's nameserver. The IP address for blog.zsec.uk is then returned to the resolver from the nameserver.
6. The DNS resolver then responds to the web browser with the IP address of the domain requested initially, and then the browser requests the IP address.

7. Finally, the server at that IP returns the webpage to be rendered in the browser, and the browser renders it.

There are four different types of server involved in loading a web page, a DNS recursor and three different name servers:

1. **DNS recursor** - A DNS recursor is designed to receive queries and lookups from applications such as web browsers. Typically the recursor is then responsible for making additional requests to satisfy the client's DNS query. For example, if you want to browse to blog.zsec.uk, a recursor will go away and make the other requests required to gain information to render and load the site. The other requests are made to the root, TLD and authoritative name servers, which are described below.
2. **Root nameserver** - The root server is the first step in translating (resolving) human readable host names into IP addresses. It is similar to an index in a library that points to different racks of books - typically it serves as a reference to other more specific locations of information.
3. **Top Level Domain(TLD) nameserver** - The top level domain server (TLD) can be thought of as a specific aisle of books in a library. This nameserver is the next step in the search for a specific IP address, and it hosts the last area of a hostname (In zsec.uk, the TLD server is "uk").
4. **Authoritative nameserver** - This final nameserver can be thought of as a dictionary on a rack of books, in which a specific name can be translated into its definition. The authoritative nameserver is the last stop in the nameserver query. If the authoritative name server has access to the requested record, it will return the IP address for the requested hostname back to the DNS Recursor (the librarian) that made the initial request.

Different Record Types

Now that we're all on the same page as to how DNS works and what it is, next up is the different types of record. Basically when you do a DNS lookup, normally, your browser will be looking for an IP address to render a site however DNS is much more feature rich. It has other types of records that can be returned based on the type of lookup.

There are a few different types of DNS record. A quick overview of each is explained in the list below.

- A: An A record specifies IP address (IPv4) for a given host. A records are used for the conversion of domain names to corresponding IP addresses.
- AAAA: Much like an A record, a AAAA (also Quad-A record) specifies IPv6 address for a given host. So it works the same way as the A record, and the difference is the type of IP address.
- CNAME: A CNAME record is like a redirector in that it specifies a domain name that has to be queried to resolve the original DNS query. Therefore CNAME records are used for creating aliases of domain names.
- TXT: A TXT record stores a variety of information but in the name, it is a text record, usually referenced for validation information or other auxiliary information about a domain. TXT records are used for protocols such as SPF, DKIM and DMARC to secure mail transfer, these are explained below.
- MX: A MX record also known as mail exchanger record, specifies the mail server responsible for accepting email messages on behalf of a domain name. Typically a domain will have a primary MX record and, in some

cases, a secondary or multiple secondary MX records for load balancing and redundancy.
- PTR: A PTR record, also known as a pointer, enables reverse DNS lookups, which are instead of lookup up a domain and getting an A record, you can look up an IP address and get a domain. It ties an IP up with a domain name. For this reason, a PTR record is often referred to as a Reverse DNS Record. The main purpose of a PTR record is primarily administrative as it confirms that an IP is in fact, used with a particular domain.
- SOA: SOA stands for start of authority, this record is typically used for administrative functions as it holds information surrounding the DNS zone information. It stores the following info;
    - Name of the server that supplied the data for the zone;
    - Administrator of the zone;
    - Current version of the data file;
    - Number of seconds a secondary name server should wait before checking for updates;
    - Number of seconds a secondary name server should wait before retrying a failed zone transfer;
    - The maximum number of seconds that a secondary name server can use data before it must either be refreshed or expire;
    - A default number of seconds for the time-to-live file on resource records.
- HINFO: The HINFO record is used less often now however, it holds information about the host CPU type and operating system. It was intended to allow protocols to optimise processing when communicating with similar peers. Currently, it is used by CloudFlare when a lookup of type ANY is issued.

There are many more DNS records but the above are the most commonly used or referred to.

Facilitating Attacks with DNS

Now that you know how this all works, next I'll touch on some of the attacks and info that an attacker can gain from DNS enumeration.

DNS Enumeration

There are a few techniques that can be leveraged to use DNS as a reconnaissance tool, these are detailed below. While these are not exploits, they leverage functionality for malicious purposes.

Zone Transfers

A zone transfer is a method that an administrator can leverage to replicate DNS databases across a group of DNS servers. The actual method for a zone transfer is perfectly fine between DNS servers as it is intended to share zones information, they can leak a lot of information that would otherwise not be available to an attacker.

While DNS records are not sensitive individually if an attacker manages to obtain a copy of the entire DNS zone for a domain, they can get a complete listing of all the hosts associated with that particular zone and thus leverage it to find interesting looking subdomains.

Subdomains

Subdomain enumeration outside of a zone transfer can be achieved by querying a DNS resolver with a list of names, and if the name is valid the resolver will show an associated DNS record. Subdomain enumeration is an essential part of conducting recon. Attackers typically map out the target's digital footprint to find weak spots such as interesting domain names or records pointing to internal hostnames that could be leveraged for accessing an internal network.

Attacking Different Records

There are many different attacks that can be carried out against specific DNS records, ranging from subdomain takeovers through to command and control over DNS. Threat actors and attackers are always looking for different new methods for attacks. A few examples of attack types include:

- Subdomain Takeovers: Takeovers work when a company has a CNAME record set up, whereby a domain; for example.zsec.uk is pointing to a content delivery network or even non-existent area, and an attacker claims the domain or area to deliver their content thus taking over the subdomain. This type of attack is often found to be used by attackers hoping to phish from internal domains, it is also found alot on bug bounty schemes and has a varying paytable.
- DNS Command and Control (C2): In the most locked-down environments, often DNS traffic should be allowed to resolve internal or external domains. As an attacker, we can leverage this as a communication channel between a target host and the command and control

server. Commands and data are included inside DNS queries and responses that hide how an attack is being conducted.
- Exfiltration: Similar to the C2 explained above, information can be exfiltrated over DNS by leveraging the TXT record; chunks of (usually base64) encoded data can be set in txt records that, when looked up by an attacker, can extract info and data from inside an organisation's network.

There are many other attacks and techniques that leverage DNS and new ones are being discovered all the time.

Hopefully, the above guide has been a handy reference point for anyone learning about the differences in records and other attacks. Part 2 of this post will follow soon, which dives into SPF, DKIM and DMARC. Like the bottom part of this post, the next post will explain what they are and how attacks can be facilitated.

Further Reading on Networking

I got into networking by following the Cisco CCNA Networking & Routing fundamentals; I'd suggest looking at the material for sure as the core fundamentals are beneficial however, the actual certification is only precious if you plan to pursue networking as a career.

Other Sources for more information can be found in the reading list below:

1. Networking Fundamentals[16]

---

[16] https://amzn.to/2GE8V9y

Follow me on Twitter https://twitter.com/ZephrFish

2. How Does the Internet Work?[17]

---

[17]https://web.stanford.edu/class/msande91si/www-spr04/readings/week1/InternetWhitepaper.htm

3. Operating Systems

When learning about information security, software development, computer science or "insert another relevant topic here" it is likely that you will come up against a variety of different operating systems. Now you might be wondering what an operating system is? The short answer is, it is the underlying software that your device runs, be this your laptop, phone, e-reader, tablet, fridge or any other appliance. It likely has an operating system.

Most new folks to this area will be primarily windows users and will have had little or no exposure to the world of Linux. Or, you might be on the other side of the fence. Having grown up with *nix by your side windows is an alien planet to you.

You might also fall into the Mac camp. Growing up with macs, you are used to things looking pretty, but have you ever tinkered with what goes on under the hood in the OS?

Do not worry if you fall into any of these three! We've all been at the same point one way or another, this next section will explain in depth some of the operating systems you might come across, and it will also show you example scenarios.

Linux

Linux is one of the most commonly used operating systems in servers & web applications to date. In 2015, Linux & Unix-like operating systems made up 98% of the servers on the Internet.

From this statistic alone, it can be seen that it's likely to be popular for a reason?

When learning about Linux, if it's new to you and you've come from a primary windows background, you'll be used to using a graphical user interface(GUI).

While Linux has a large variety of GUIs, it excels most with its use of the Terminal. The command-line interface, sometimes referred to as the CLI or Terminal, is a tool to type text commands to perform specific tasks in contrast to the mouse's pointing and clicking on menus and buttons.

You may have come across the command line within windows before(cmd.exe). If this is something you've never come across, you're still probably scratching your head thinking:

What the heck is a terminal or command line?

Allow me to explain some more since you can directly control the computer by typing, many tasks can be performed more quickly. As a result of this, some tasks can be automated with special commands that loop through and perform the same action on many files saving you, potentially, loads of time in the process.

The application or user interface that accepts your typed responses and displays the data on the screen is called a shell, and there are many different varieties that you can choose from, but the most common these days is the Bash shell, which is the default on Linux and Mac systems in the Terminal application.

Getting started with the command line interface

Many of the folk I've spoken to have been interested in the command line but haven't really known where to get started. I'd usually say just fire up Linux and play. However, for some people, this might be a mentally challenging task, for those of you who want a little hand on your way, I suggest you take a Command Line Crash Course[18] on Code Academy.

For those of you who know the basics, I suggest you start to look at bash scripting to enable you to do things. The simplest bash script would be a hello world application, as shown in the code below:

```
#!/bin/bash
echo "Hello World"
```

Open this in a text editor such as nano, vim, leafpad (if you prefer a GUI) and save as myscript.sh. Some of you will see the above code and think WHAT EVEN IS THAT, I DON'T UNDERSTAND, HEEEELLLLLPPPPPPP. And others might see it and think I sort of know what that does but tell me more. Don't worry if you're in either of these two situations, and I'm about to explain what it does, what else you can do.

For the first camp of people who see the code and are running about confused and crying. Do not worry; it's going to be all right. Firstly, explaining that the lines of code do, the first line #!/bin/bash describes the environment that the script is running, which is the shell environment in Linux = bash[19]. The following line is a simple print Hello world on screen.

---

[18]https://www.codecademy.com/learn/learn-the-command-line
[19]https://en.wikipedia.org/wiki/Bash_(Unix_shell)

Follow me on Twitter https://twitter.com/ZephrFish

Now, this may be too simple for some of you, for those of you who want to get more out of things, pick a project and write it in bash, check out http://www.commandlinefu.com/ for tips and tricks of things to do. If you're stuck for ideas, check out my Github[20] scripts.

This should be enough to get you started on Linux; there will be a future more in-depth write-up on advanced topics to check out. Onwards!

Windows

Windows is one of the most commonly used operating systems in the world, in comparison to Linux, it is lesser used in security; however still an OS of choice for many. The possibilities for usage are pretty extensive, the UI is usable and the support of tools is varied however, by default supports virtualisation via 3rd party applications and is easy to setup.

PowerShell

PowerShell is one of two (three[21] if you're on Windows 10 and have the bash environment setup) terminal interfaces on Windows, it serves as a tool to facilitate automation & other exploitation on.

PowerShell can be used to create scripts similar to bash scripting on Unix, however the syntax and coding is very similar to that of Perl. It has come out as a powerful tool for hacking & post-exploitation as many anti-virus and anti-malware

---
[20]https://github.com/ZephrFish/RandomScripts
[21]https://www.howtogeek.com/249966/how-to-install-and-use-the-linux-bash-shell-on-windows-10/

programs don't catch it due to the execution methods. Some brilliant frameworks and exploit tools have been built based upon PowerShell. Feel free to check them out.

- Empire[22]
- PoshC2[23]
- Powersploit[24]

In a security sense, post-exploitation techniques aren't the only use for PowerShell. It can also be used for legitimate system administration purposes to allow you to gain information about the system or systems on a network, and it has endless potential for automating mundane tasks within Windows such as deployment[25] and GPO[26].

It also acts as the primary modern command-line interface within windows, facilitating other programming languages such as python or ruby. It is accessible by doing the following ctrl + r then typing PowerShell, this will launch you into a PowerShell session with a prompt; this prompt will accept a certain degree of *nix commands as ls and echo.

You can find out all of the commands available within the PowerShell world by using the man or help commands against any command or module. However, before you do this, you'll want to run update-help to ensure all of the manual and help pages are up to date.

Accessing PowerShell is as simple as windows key + r, then typing powershell.exe. This will pop a PowerShell window open.

---

[22] https://github.com/BC-SECURITY/Empire
[23] https://github.com/nettitude/PoshC2
[24] https://github.com/PowerShellMafia/PowerSploit
[25] https://github.com/PSAppDeployToolkit/PSAppDeployToolkit
[26] https://technet.microsoft.com/en-gb/library/ee461027.aspx

---

Follow me on Twitter https://twitter.com/ZephrFish

From this interface, you have direct access to the underlying operating system and PowerShell cmdlets, which are modules built into PowerShell that have different functions.

Command Line (CMD.exe)

Another terminal environment built into windows is the command line tool (cmd.exe), it acts as a more dated PowerShell instance. It does not support modules but still gives access to underlying system commands to find out about files and other aspects of the operating system.

The prompt varies slightly in cmd vs PowerShell. However, the basic core commands work the same on both. Try it yourself, type `whoami` in cmd first, then try the same in PowerShell.

Knowing your way around both PowerShell and cmd is very useful for post-exploitation in testing and general usage. I'd suggest having a read into batch & PowerShell scripting better to understand both `ps` & `cmd`.

A fundamental batch script is shown below, it prints out some text to the screen and creates a folder, then explains to the user what it just did. You can try too by saving this into a `.bat` file then double-clicking on the `.bat` to run it.

```
1  @echo off
2
3  :: do stuff
4  echo Hello World
5  mkdir hello-world
6
7  :: Explain what the script just did
8  echo:
9  echo Created hello-world folder
10 echo:
11
12 end local
13
14 :: Pause allowing the user to read what shit does
15 pause
```

To do similar on PowerShell a script such as the following can be created:

```
1  # PowerShell Hello World
2  Write-Host
3  Write-Host 'Hello World!'
4  mkdir hello-world-ps
```

Then to run it on our host, we need to do a few minor things within PowerShell. First the execution policy needs to be set for the current user to execute the script. Then our script can be run.

```
1  PS C:\Desktop\PoC> Set-ExecutionPolicy -ExecutionPo\
2  licy Unrestricted -Scope CurrentUser
3
4  Execution Policy Change
5  The execution policy helps protect you from scripts\
6   that you do not trust. Changing the execution poli\
7  cy might expose
8  you to the security risks described in the about_Ex\
9  ecution_Policies help topic at
10 http://go.microsoft.com/fwlink/?LinkID=135170. Do y\
11 ou want to change the execution policy?
12 [Y] Yes  [A] Yes to All  [N] No  [L] No to All  [S]\
13  Suspend  [?] Help (default is "N"): Y
14 PS C:\Desktop\PoC> cat .\ps.ps1
15 # PowerShell Hello World
16 Write-Host 'Hello World!'
17 mkdir hello-world-ps
18 PS C:\Desktop\PoC> .\ps
19 Hello World!
20
21
22      Directory: C:\Desktop\PoC
23
24
25 Mode                LastWriteTime         Length Na\
26 me
27 ----                -------------         ------ --\
28 --
29 d-----        15/04/2017     10:56                he\
30 llo-world-ps
```

PowerShell has an execution policy in place by default to protect users from themselves, it prevents scripts from running to stop malicious things from happening.

Bash on Windows

What is this witchcraft you may wonder? Well as of Windows 10, it is now possible to run bash on windows from the inbuilt OS rather than install a 3rd party simulator such as Cygwin or PentestBox. To enable it the following steps can be taken:

1. Turn Developer Mode on via Settings > Update & security > For developers
2. Click the Start button , click Control Panel, click Programs, and click Turn Windows features on or off.
3. Enable Windows Subsystem for Linux
4. You can also install different Linux OSes from the Microsoft store, including Ubuntu, Debian and Kali!

Once this is done, you should be able to open cmd or PowerShell and type "bash" this will drop you into the bash environment, which is running Ubuntu. It has all of the standard features you'd expect to see in Linux.

Allowing for package installation, bash scripting, built-in SSH and more. The only things I've had minor trouble with is packages that require raw access to the network such as nmap and masscan, however, there are windows variants available for these anyway!

Now to show a bash script running within Windows, I wrote the following quick script:

```
1  #!/bin/bash
2  whoami
3  id
4  pwd
5  echo "Hello World"
6  mkdir bashonwindows
```

As simple as that, show what user you are, what your privileges are echo a message to the Terminal then create me a folder.

Tooling

Alongside the terminal environments, there are a lot of tools designed for use within windows. Lots of common tools within Linux have been ported to windows too such as nmap & metasploit both of which are used a lot in infrastructure type penetration testing.

The two areas in which tooling is most prevalent on windows appears to be reporting & exploit development/debugging which sees a lot of tools and debuggers out there for use.

Under the UI

For a lot of readers Windows might well be your daily driver, so you'll be used to the way in which the user interface works, however you might not be aware of how under the hood works. Have you ever done `windows key + r` then `regedit`? If not, this opens the registry editor for windows, think of this like the real bits and bobs under the prettiness of windows, similar to `ls -aliRtu /` on *unix.

Follow me on Twitter https://twitter.com/ZephrFish

MacOS

MacOS or OSX as it's sometimes known is a Unix based system(BSD) which has commodities that are both similar to Windows & Linux. Being Unix based it shares the same core terminal as Linux(BASH).

It is proprietary and closed source in comparison to Linux and other Unix variants. What it does have however is a massive market share, it is exclusive to Macbooks and Apple Mac computers (with the exception of hackintoshes[27]). The functionality from a security standpoint is more or less the same as Linux.

The added benefit of using a Mac mainly being that it has a UNIX based OS out of the box, supports virtualisation and they tend to look pretty sleek.

---
[27]https://www.hackintosh.com

4. Virtualisation

This section talks about what virtualisation is, why it is important and how it works. I will also take you through setting up your first virtual machine (VM) in both VMWare & Virtual Box.

What is Virtualisation?

Virtualisation put briefly is the process of creating a container of resources to run an operating system within the context of another. Think of it like building a shed in your house and setting it up like another house or living environment.

What it is Used For

Virtualisation is all about separating traditional IT resources into more easily managed and centralised solutions. This separation often increases scalability, improves resource utilisation, and reduces administrative resources.

Specifically, it works by utilising hardware to create a virtual environment similar to that of a physical machine, taking an example as you have a desktop that has a quad core processor, 4 GB of ram & a 500GB Hard drive.

In the conventional way you could install windows on this and roll with a single operating system however say you need to do something in Linux or another OS, you could dual boot systems but the quicker way to do so would be to virtualise.

Setting Up Your First Virtual Machine

For this section you'll need to download either VMWare player OR Virtual Box, both work just the same. My personal preference is VMWare Workstation (paid for version) as it has some neat features such as export and snapshots plus other little tweaks here and there.

Note: I'm going to show you how to setup on windows, however to do so on Mac & Linux is more or less the same with both VMWare & Virtual box.

Steps to Create a VM

- **Step 1**: Obtain from VMWare[28] or VirtualBox[29]
- **Step 2**: Obtain an ISO for an OS you want to virtualise; for this tutorial I'll be using Debian[30], however you can use whatever OS you want. ####Create a new VM (VMWare)
    - *VMWare*: Select File>New Virtual Machine
    - *VMWare*: This will spawn a new VM wizard, from here select "Installer disk image file" (ISO) and choose the ISO you want to use to setup a VM.
    - *VMWare*: Follow the wizard though select the appropriate operating system to match the ISO you've selected.
    - *VMWare*: Give it a name and a location on your local machine.

---

[28]https://my.vmware.com/en/web/vmware/free#desktop_end_user_computing/vmware_workstation_player/12_0
[29]https://www.virtualbox.org/wiki/Downloads
[30]https://www.debian.org/CD/http-ftp/#stable

Follow me on Twitter https://twitter.com/ZephrFish

- *VMWare*: Select the specs you require, depending on what purpose you want for the machine you're creating.
- *VMWare*: Once this is done it's just a case of starting your VM by clicking the green start button, then it's just a case of setting up like you would an OS normally.

Create a new VM (Virtual Box)

- Once you have Virtual box open, creating a VM is fairly simple. Simply click New, to create a new VM.
- Next select Expert Mode which should give a window similar to that shown below. This allows you to name your new VM, select the OS you're installing, the version & specify the amount of RAM you want to give it too. In this example I'm going to install Debian with 2GB of RAM.
  - Click Create
  - Select the size & location you want to store the virtual drive file.
  - Then select Create again.

Once this is done VirtualBox will create an instance of your VM, the final step is to click start, and give the VM an ISO to install.

Other Platforms

There are many other platforms too for virtualisation of operating systems, I've simply demonstrated the two most common applications used on consumer devices. Some examples worth checking out can be seen in the list below.

- ESXi
- HyperV
- Xen
- KVM
- QEMU

5. Programming

In security it can be very useful to understand programming, whilst you might not be able to code straight away it is very useful to understand the core fundamentals.

Throughout my blog and this book, I am hoping to give you the basics to prepare you to start your journey in learning the different paths of security & hacking.

This section will cover off logic, programming basics, the differences between language types and some tips on starting points in coding.

To start with I'm going to explain basic logic through the use of truth tables. Now some of you may not know the first thing about logic and may have never even heard of what a truth table is, however do not worry it will all be clear soon.

Logic

Logic is the understanding of whether something is true or false, how it works any why it's correct or incorrect. Outside of programming one will deal with logic on a daily basis sometimes without even realising.

To start with I'm going to explain basic logic through the use of truth tables. A truth table is a mathematical table used in logic. This is the idea of one (1) being true and zero (0) being false which is also known as on and off.

Very basic logic has three main logic gates: and, or, not. Each serve as an operator in a logic statement, the three sections explain what each does and how it works.

And

At a very basic level the and logic operator works with one value AND another equal the third, there are four possible outcomes with this. These are explained below:

Value	Value2	Equals
0	0	0
0	1	0
1	0	0
1	1	1

Essentially both values need to be True for the end result to be True. This is useful in programming if a statement or function is being made where two arguments need to be present before continuing. Think for example if you write a program that prints out someone's name and age. The inputs are both required in order to print out the result, the following example pseudo code shows this in the form of an if, else loop.

```
1  If name & address are true:
2  print "My name is" + $NAME + "and I am" + $AGE "yea\
3  rs old..."
4  else:
5  print "Error, name AND age values required"
```

If you don't follow, essentially it is saying if value x & value y are present like the bottom line of the truth table above then print out the statement "My name is bob and I am 18 years old..." where $NAME is Bob and $AGE is 18 otherwise print the statement "`Error, name AND age values required`" to the screen.

Or

Similar to the and operator, OR also requires a minimum of two inputs for it to produce an output. The difference being with OR is that it does not require both values to be true for the end result to be true, the following table demonstrates this point:

Value	Value2	Equals
0	0	0
0	1	1
1	0	1
1	1	1

As can be clearly seen as long as there is a True value (1) in the equation the resulting output will be true, only when both values are false will the end result be false.

Not

The not operator works in a different way to and and or as it only has two possible outcomes, 1 & 0 or true & false. Essentially if one value is presented as an input the output will be the inverse of it.

Input	Output
0	1
1	0

Logic operators are used a lot in different programming

languages, the main example of this in security being related to web applications and database queries such as SQL (Structured Query Language).

An example query might look similar to `SELECT * FROM Users WHERE FirstName equals Bob AND LastName equals Smith` where the query is selecting all users with the first and last name matching `Bob Smith` this demonstrates the use of the AND logic operator in a query language such as SQL.

And, Or & Not are the main basic logic operators however there are a few others, feel free to check these out: `AND`, `OR`, `XOR`, `NOT`, `NAND`, `NOR` and `XNOR`.

The Basics - Functions, Variables, Learning

Alongside logic the other aspects used a lot in programming are functions & variables, almost all languages both compiled and scripting use functions and variables to do some thing or another.

Variables

What is a variable really? A variable is a value within a program that can change, depending on conditions or on information passed to the program. A variable usually holds information that is used later in the program or referred to for other actions.

Usually, a program or application consists of a list of instructions that tell the computer what to do and data that the application uses when it is running. The data consists of constants or fixed values that never change and variable values (which are usually initialized to "0" or another default value because the actual values will be supplied by a program's user).

Typically, both constants, and variables are defined as certain data types. Each data type limits the form of the data. Examples of data types include: an integer expressed as a decimal number or a string of characters, usually limited in length. There are many different data types across all of the languages available however as a standard typically strings and integers are available at the very least.

Functions

A function is a piece of code usually which utilises various services or actions that can be used over and over again by calling the piece of code. An example of this might be if I set a function named pow() and each time pow is run it prints out the letters x,y & z. This might look like something similar to the function below:

```
function pow()
{
    print "x,y & z"
}

pow
```

The code above sets up the function pow() and whenever pow is referenced after that function, the application prints out "x,y & z" to the terminal.

In many programming languages there is access to a compiler which contains a set of pre-made functions that a programmer can specify by writing language statements. These provided functions are sometimes referred to as library routines. Some functions are self-sufficient and can return results to the requesting program without help. Other functions need to make requests of the operating system in order to perform their work. Essentially functions are very important when writing code as they save you time.

Language Types

When dealing in security you're most likely to come across two different types of programming language; compiled & scripting. There are many other types to check out too if you're interested here is a link[31] to Wikipedia that lists a large majority.

The following subheadings summarise the different languages you can learn in each category however if you want a more inclusive list of learning resources check out programming motherfucker... do you speak it?[32].

Scripting

The main scripting languages & environments that you will come up against first hand is likely to be PowerShell or bash depending on what operating system you use as a base. Both of which have already been discussed in Chapter 3: Operating Systems. However, if you'd like to learn more about either, check out the links: bash[33] or PowerShell[34].

---

[31] https://en.wikipedia.org/wiki/List_of_programming_languages_by_type
[32] http://programming-motherfucker.com/become.html
[33] https://learncodethehardway.org/unix/
[34] https://blogs.technet.microsoft.com/heyscriptingguy/2015/01/04/weekend-scripter-the-best-ways-to-learn-powershell/

Follow me on Twitter https://twitter.com/ZephrFish

Other than the two pre-built into the OS, there are many other languages that are classed as scripting. The three most common that I've seen in hacking/InfoSec tend to be: python, ruby & Perl. All of which have different purposes and share different tools being written in them.

Some tools you might have heard of that have been written in one of the three are as follows Perl - Nikto[35], Python - SQLMap[36], Ruby - Metasploit[37]

Specifically, when breaking into the field I'd recommend looking into learning python as it is a very useful language to not only be able to write in but to also be able to read. In order to pick it up and learn I'd suggest Learn Python the Hardway[38], this will give you a solid basic understanding.

However, if books arenâ€™t your thing you should also check out Python on CodeAcademy[39] this will take you through interactive exercises to test your ability to learn. Once you have the basics nailed down I'd highly suggest checking out Violent Python[40] & Black Hat Python[41] both of which give python a backing in the security field with different things to try out and build.

If all else fails, try picking a project to better understand the language; it doesn't need to be security related! The first project I created in Python was an app to calculate whether getting a cinema pass for the month was worth it for you or not. It would take an input of the films you want to see then, work out if it was better value for money to get the pass or

---

[35] https://github.com/sullo/nikto
[36] http://sqlmap.org/
[37] https://www.rapid7.com/products/metasploit/
[38] https://learnpythonthehardway.org/book/
[39] https://www.codecademy.com/learn/python
[40] http://amzn.to/2qGH1jm
[41] http://amzn.to/2qQHtIm

Follow me on Twitter https://twitter.com/ZephrFish

just to pay per time.

I put a poll out on twitter to find out what people felt was the most difficult aspect of programming and the result that came out on top was lack of ideas - as an answer to that, try having a look at netsec[42] & hacking[43] on reddit and try to create or recreate some of the tools published on there to allow you to better understand creation of things.

Compiled

Another type of language you're likely to come across is a compiled one, the most common example of this is C and the different flavours of C(C/C++/C#). A lot of exploits & tools are written in C as it's a fast programming language, it also has many build in features allowing for usage of loads of functions.

The main difference between a scripting language and a compiled one is that a scripting language can be written in any text editor and is interpreted. Whereas a compiled language requires the use of a compiler to run in a compiled state. A few examples of scripting vs compiled languages are shown in the list below:

Scripting Languages

- Python
- Ruby
- Perl
- Lua
- JavaScript

---

[42]https://www.reddit.com/r/netsec
[43]https://www.reddit.com/r/hacking

Compiled Languages

- C
- C++
- C#
- D
- Java
- .Net

Starting out if you've already tried out python and, are hungry to learn more I'd suggest having a look at C. It isn't my strongest language, but I can read it and modify where needed.

As a minimum being able to read programming is a must when it comes to hacking. Often exploits and tools will be written in different languages and may need tweaking before they will work - having the ability to spot where things need changed or being able to google the correct questions will stand you in good stead.

As far as learning is concerned much like python, C also has many learning resources the link above(programming-motherfucker[44]) gives many routes to the same end goal however I've found learn C the hard way[45] to be a good resource.

Other than this you can try jumping in at the deep end and going for a project, if you've learned the basics with python, you'll find C slightly easier to learn in comparison to other compiled languages.

---
[44] http://programming-motherfucker.com/
[45] https://learncodethehardway.org/c/

6. Infrastructure

Infrastructure penetration testing (also known as network penetration testing by some) like web application testing, is probably one of the most common forms of assessment anyone starting out in the industry is going to come across both in the consultancy sector and in the world of bug bounties.

It is also the main focus of offensive security's pentesting with kali[46] course. The main aim of infrastructure hacking is to find flaws at the network level of a target - be this on the internal network inside the firewall or external perimeter.

Like web apps, infrastructure assessments encompass many factors too including:

- Port Security
- Service Security
- Password Security
- Different Protocols
- Firewalls/Intrusion Detection Systems/Intrusion Prevention System
- Network Equipment: such as routers, switches & firewalls
- Other segments of networks such as VPNs and endpoint devices

Following this rough outline, a baseline methodology can be taken as information gathering, scanning based upon info

---

[46]https://www.offensive-security.com/information-security-training/penetration-testing-training-kali-linux/

Follow me on Twitter https://twitter.com/ZephrFish

gathered during recon, exploiting vulnerabilities found from scanning then pivoting across systems & persisting on penetrated ones.

The headings below explain the stages of this methodology in more detail and outline some tooling to take a look at for each stage. Note that some tooling will only be applicable for internal network testing as this usually assumes you will be on a client network and have access to 'private IP addresses' - class A, B & C network addresses: e.g. similar to 10.x.x.x, 172.16.x.x, 192.168.x.x.

Reconnaissance

Before you even start to look at a target the first step is to carry out some reconnaissance. Usually this can be done entirely passively to begin with i.e. no port scanning or traffic sent directly to the IP address or host. The main aim of reconnaissance in any operation/assessment is to gain as much information about the target(s) as possible to aid you later on in the process.

Discovery

Arguably the most important first stage in recon is to carry out open source intelligence gathering in order to discover links to the target organisation & other potentially interesting points.

Passive Information Gathering is the process of collecting information about your target using publicly available information. This is the main methodology that open source intelligence gathering follows as the main aim is to gather as much information about your target without actually sending traffic directly to the target domain or organisation.

This could include services like search engine results, whois information, background check services, public company information, current and past employees' information and much more.

An example might be that you've been tasked with testing domain.com however the client has stated that other subdomains would be of interest and may be added to scope.

Using open source intelligence, you might be able to discover admin.uat.domain.com and identify it has a gaping vulnerability that could leave the client open to attack. By appending this to your report you have alerted the client to a potential vulnerable entry point.

The client responds by adding it into scope and you identify a remote code execution exploit allowing you full control over the server, had you not done some digging you might have never found this and thus good preparation is always a good start.

Another aspect of discovery passively can be done via using google dorks[47] to identify IP ranges and other interesting hosts. This also falls under passive analysis up until you make any connections to the IPs or browse to domains.

Alongside google dorks there are many great free tools that can be used to gather information about a target all of which use open source intel to build up a picture about your target. The short list below outlines a few I'd recommend checking out.

General Recon

---
[47]https://www.exploit-db.com/google-hacking-database/

- Spiderfoot
- Maltego
- Recon-NG

Domain Enumeration

- Subbrute
- Sublist3r
- Knockpy
- DNS Parallel Prober
- theharvester
- fierce

Google Dorks to Try

- site:*.domain.com -www
- site:..domain.com -www
- site:*.domain.com ext:pdf
- site:*.domain.com ext:php

Most of the tooling above takes the approach of a combination of passive and active intel gathering, the general recon tools have options to do 100% passive or some active to discover the most information. All of these techniques are both applicable to penetration testing & bug bounties however it should be noted all analysis should be carried out inline with the scope and requirements set out by your client.

Spiderfoot

Spiderfoot[48] is a framework written in python that can be used for open source intelligence gathering automation. It works off of being given a domain or a company name and then leverages modules to identify where the domain or company is referenced, this combined with some comparison tools built in allows for a decent footprint analysis to be carried out against a target.

It has many modes that can be selected from simply passive with a stealthy approach so as to not raise any alarms that a target is being looked into vs full on active mode which encompasses many search engines, tools, APIs, websites and many more to find out info about said target. I'm not going to go into how to set it up and run however it is mostly self-explanatory simply download and run then go to `localhost:5001` in a browser to access the web interface. For more information about spiderfoot check out the documentation on their website[49].

Maltego

Maltego[50] is in many ways much like spiderfoot however instead of being written in python and accessible via a web interface, maltego is written in java and has a fully fledged GUI. By default, Kali Linux has the community version installed however you can download and run it on other OSes too. I am no expert on the usage of it however have found that the transforms built in do a great job of basic analysis of a target. Transforms by the way are like modules they lean on other services to identify information.

---

[48] http://www.spiderfoot.net
[49] http://www.spiderfoot.net/documentation/
[50] https://www.paterva.com/web7/

Follow me on Twitter https://twitter.com/ZephrFish

Each transform will identify more information about your target and you can simply right click on each new node and select run more transforms, from doing this more information can be discovered. For more information about maltego check out their wiki[51].

Recon-NG

Recon-NG[52] is like the metasploit of OSINT, it has many plugins and modules allowing for a vast degree of different information gathering techniques. From the website overview about Recon-NG it was designed exclusively for web-based open source reconnaissance.

Like spiderfoot it is 100% open source allowing for new modules to be written for it and actively developed. It can help you a lot when looking at individuals, domains and companies. Definitely check out the wiki for it here[53] to learn more about the different modules and features.

Domain Enumeration

When it comes to subdomain identification and DNS bruteforcing there are some great tools for achieving this goal. All of the tools in the next few subsections can be used to identify sub domains for better recon and to help you grow the attack surface.

---

[51]https://www.paterva.com/web7/docs/documentation.php
[52]https://bitbucket.org/LaNMaSteR53/recon-ng
[53]https://bitbucket.org/LaNMaSteR53/recon-ng/wiki/Home

Subbrute & Sublist3r

Subbrute[54] & Sublist3r[55] both written in python use a variety of brute-force techniques to identify subdomains. They can be very useful if you've been tasked with testing *.domain.com and you want to find out some potential targets other than just the main domain. Sublist3r in particular uses several sources to identify domains and outputs these to the terminal. An example of this running against a target is shown below:

```
# python sublist3r.py -d zerosec.co.uk -o zerosec
                 ____          _     _ _     _   _____
     _          / ___| _   _| |__ | (_)___| |_|___ / _ __
    / _ \      \___ \| | | | '_ \| | / __| __| |_ \| '__|
    \/ '_|      ___) | |_| | |_) | | \__ \ |_ ___) | |
     | |       |____/ \__,_|_.__/|_|_|___/\__|____/|_|
    /|_|

                # Coded By Ahmed Aboul-Ela - @aboul\
3la

[-] Enumerating subdomains now for zerosec.co.uk
[-] Searching now in Baidu..
[-] Searching now in Yahoo..
[-] Searching now in Google..
[-] Searching now in Bing..
[-] Searching now in Ask..
[-] Searching now in Netcraft..
```

---

[54]https://github.com/TheRook/subbrute
[55]https://github.com/aboul3la/Sublist3r

```
22  [-] Searching now in DNSdumpster..
23  [-] Searching now in Virustotal..
24  [-] Searching now in ThreatCrowd..
25  [-] Searching now in SSL Certificates..
26  [-] Searching now in PassiveDNS..
27  [-] Saving results to file: zerosec
28  [-] Total Unique Subdomains Found: 1
29  www.zerosec.co.uk
```

As can be seen from the output the tool looks at several sources in order to try and identify different subdomains, in this example I have used a domain I own: `zerosec.co.uk`. Sublist3r utilizes subbrute as a module used to scan however subbrute can be used on its own too which produces outputs like so:

```
1  # python subbrute.py zerosec.co.uk
2  zerosec.co.uk
3  www.zerosec.co.uk
```

Again this produces only one subdomain which is www notice the output for sub brute is slightly less verbose as its main usage is for purely brute-forcing, it does not leverage any other sources.

Knockpy

Knockpy[56] works in a similar way to sublist3r as it uses brute-force and heuristic techniques to identify sub-domains. It works from a baseline wordlist and iterates through this in order to find targets. Additionally, it also features checking

---

[56]https://github.com/guelfoweb/knock

for zone transfers in DNS & checking for wildcard DNS. These both are features that fierce[57] shares. To setup knockpy, simply clone it down from Github then install it with `python setup.py install`. From here usage is really simply just `knock domain.com` and it will do its stuff.

DNS Parallel Prober

DNS Parallel Prober[58] or as I seem to have started calling it, DNS Queue was written and developed by two of my friends and colleagues; Lorenzo[59] & Kyle[60]. It is essentially a proof of concept for a parallelised domain name prober. It creates a queue of threads and tasks each one to probe a sub-domain of the given root domain. At every iteration step each dead thread is removed and the queue is replenished as necessary.

What this means is that, it is great at identifying subdomains based off of a wordlist. This is thanks to a great wordlist that I supplied, it does an excellent job at finding some that the other tools struggle with especially the awkwardly named or even sub-subdomains. The setup and running of this tool is very simple as a quick start simply clone it down from Github, install the dependencies then run:

`dns-queue.py example.com 100 out.txt -i subdomains.txt`

Where `example.com` is the target domain, `100` is the amount of threads, `out.txt` is the output file and `-i subdomains.txt` is the wordlist you want to use. As simple as that and you're away!

---

[57] http://tools.kali.org/information-gathering/fierce
[58] https://github.com/lorenzog/dns-parallel-prober
[59] https://github.com/lorenzog
[60] https://twitter.com/kylefleming217

theharvester

Alongside DNS enumeration and subdomain discovery, another form of intelligence gathering that can be useful is the identification of email addresses. This is where theharvester[61] comes into its own, designed originally for crawling search engines for emails it has grown arms and legs to enable you to find out information about a target domain, find email addresses, PGP keys, subdomains & virtual hosts on the same IP space as the target. Example usage when looking at a domain might look similar to this:

```
1    theharvester -d zerosec.co.uk -b all -l 1000
```

Where the target domain is zerosec.co.uk, the listing target is all available i.e. google, Bing, PGP, etc. The listing limit is 1000 to look through pages and results.

Google Dorks aka Google Hacking

Google Dorks also known as google hacking is a technique using advanced search operators to extract information from google. There is a database that has been created over the years full of different search terms to uncover juicy information, this is located at GHDB[62]. Paired with the other OSINT techniques explained above google dorks can be very powerful and useful when profiling a target, they can serve as a fantastic stepping stone for uncovering those extra little bits of information to make a fuller picture of your target. Additionally, they fall into the passive category as you're purely viewing search results, it only touches upon active when you visit the site.

---

[61]https://github.com/laramies/theHarvester
[62]https://www.offensive-security.com/community-projects/google-hacking-database/

Follow me on Twitter https://twitter.com/ZephrFish

Scanning

After conducting some in depth intelligence gathering hopefully if it has been successful you will have a collection of domains or IP addresses to start looking at. Now the fun part where passive analysis moves over to active. This is where you utilize port scanning, service enumeration & vulnerability analysis in order to discover entry points to the target network.

A port scan is a method for determining which ports on a network are open. Think of the ports of a network like the windows and doors of a house. The act of port scanning can be thought of like knocking on doors to see if someone is home. Running a port scan on a network or server reveals which ports are open and listening (receiving information), as well as revealing the presence of security devices such as firewalls that are present between the sender and the target. This technique is known as fingerprinting.

There are many tools out there for port scanning however the most famous and commonly used one is called nmap[63]. Nmap ("Network Mapper") is an open source and free tool for network discovery and security scanning. It isn't only for hacking purposes, it has genuine use cases by network administrators for identifying which ports certain servers have open & what services are listening on them.

Over the past decade, nmap has grown arms and legs. As a result, it is much more now than just a port scanner, it is possible to find open ports, profile services, fingerprint vulnerabilities and conduct vulnerability scanning all from one tool! I'd suggest checking out the nmap site for more

---

[63] https://nmap.org

Follow me on Twitter https://twitter.com/ZephrFish

information on the full capabilities of nmap however theoretically it is entirely possible to use only nmap and metasploit for an engagement given their mass amount of modules & capabilities!

There are many options when it comes to nmap and port scanning in general, a lot of variables and flags can come into play, the line below is a typical scan that I might run against a target:

```
1  nmap -sSV -p- -iL targets.txt -oA output_syn --min-\
2  parallelism 64 --min-hostgroup 96 -T4 --version-all\
3   --reason --open
```

Now what does this do you might be wondering? Here's what each flag means and why I've included it:

- -sSV - Makes nmap carry out a SYN Scan meaning that it only sends a syn command to the target if the server responds with a SYN/ACK (synchronization acknowledged) packet from a particular port, it means the port is open. The V flag means carry out a version scan of the open ports that nmap discovers.
- -p- - Instructs nmap to scan all 65535 ports (1-65535), you can also use -p 0-65535 to include port 0, which in very rare cases will return as open however nothing runs on it by default.
- -iL - This flag allows nmap to take an input file containing either domains or IP addresses.
- -oA - Outputs the scan results to the three available formats: .xml, .nmap, .gnmap.
- --min-parallelism 64 - Specifies the minimum amount of parallel processes at one time. This combined with

`--min-hostgroup 96` are both performance flags[64] for nmap.

- `--min-hostgroup 96` - Specifies the minimum amount of hosts to scan in a group.
- `-T4` - Specifies a more specific form of timing performance which tunes up more of the flags for timeouts and more.
- `--version-all` - Sends additional probes in order to identify a more specific version of the service running on an open port.
- `--reason` - Forces nmap to print out the reason as to why a port was determined as open, all going well this should be SYN/ACK as the reason.
- `--open` - Selects to only show open ports, I use this on and off depending on what I am scanning.

There are many more combinations that I will use across tests however I'll leave it up to you to try out some of the other options, the man page holds all of the available flags and what each does.

Nmap or Network mapper is an open source tool for network discovery and security analysis. It is used by many people in different job roles, from system administrators to penetration testers to developers and everyone inbetween. The primary uses are network discovery and analysis.

Nmap uses raw IP packets to determine what hosts are available on a network,it can also be used to identify what services (application name and version), operating system verions, what filters/firewalls are in use, and dozens of other characteristics.

---

[64]https://nmap.org/book/man-performance.html

Nmap runs on all major computer operating systems, and official binary packages are available for Linux, Windows, and Mac OS X. Typically nmap is used on the command line by calling `nmap` however there is also a GUI available in the form of `zenmap`.

In addition to the core tooling the nmap suite also includes a netcat-like tool on steroids(ncat), scan results comparison (Ndiff), and a packet generation and response analysis tool (Nping).

Port Scanning?

Port scanning is the act systematically scanning a computer's ports/services. Since a port is a place where information goes in and out of a computer, port scanning identifies openings into a computer. Port scanning has legitimate uses in managing networks, system administration and other network based tasks. However it can also be malicious in nature if someone is looking for a weakened access point to break into a system.

Typically it is one of the first techniques used to identify weaknesses or footholds into a network. One thing to note though is that the act of port scanning does fall under active recon and will send traffic to a target rather than passive scanning using things like OSINT.

Port States

Before we dive into the different flags, it is worth understanding that when scanning a port can have three states and depending on the scan type will depend on why the state has been returned. The main three are:

- Open: Open means that an application or service is listening for connections or traffic on the on the target system.
- Closed: Closed ports have no application listening on them. Ports are classified as unfiltered when they are responsive to Nmap's probes, but Nmap cannot determine whether they are open or closed.
- Filtered: Filtered means that a firewall, filter, or other network obstacle is blocking the port so that Nmap cannot tell whether it is open or closed.

Nmap reports other state combinations such as `open|filtered` and `closed|filtered` when it cannot determine which of the two states describe a port.

Some Common Commands

Nmap is one of the most used tools when carrying out infrastructure-like engagements. As such there are many different flags and command combinations that can be used to identify weaknesses and interesting information about hosts. The following sets of commands can be used to scan different types of hosts, each flag is explained and has been tuned for maximum performance.

Basic Scanning Options

There are three fairly commmon flags used in nmap for types of scanning, these are TCP connect scans, SYN & UDP. The flags for thes are shown below and a brief explanation of how they work is included too:

- -sT: TCP connect scan is the default TCP scan type when SYN scan is not an option. This is selected when a user doesn't have elevate priveleges on a machine and therefore does not have permission to send raw packets or is scanning IPv6 networks. Instead of writing raw packets as most other scan types do, Nmap asks the underlying operating system to establish a connection with the target machine and port by issuing the connect system call and a TCP three way handshake. This is the same high-level system call that web browsers, P2P clients, and most other network-enabled applications use to establish a connection.
- -sS: This flag is a SYN scan and it is the default, most popular scan option when using nmap. It can be performed quickly, scanning thousands of ports per second on a fast network or modern network. SYN scaning is relatively unobtrusive and stealthy, since it does not complete the TCP handshake, rather it sends syn and waits for a syn-ack response. Based on the response the port will then come back as either open, closed or filtered:

Probe Response	Assigned State
TCP SYN/ACK response	`open`
TCP RST response	`closed`
No response received or ICMP unreachable errors	`filtered`

- -sU: UDP scan works by sending a UDP packet to every targeted port. For most ports, this packet will be empty (no payload), but for a few of the more common ports a protocol-specific payload will be sent. Based on the response, or lack thereof, the port is assigned to one of four states as detailed in the table below:

Probe Response	Assigned State
Any UDP response from target port	`open`
No response received after retransmission	`open|filtered`
ICMP port unreachable error (type 3, code 3)	`closed`
Other ICMP unreachable errors (type 3, code 1, 2, 9, 10, or 13)	`filtered`

- `-sV: Version scan`, this will probe specific services and try to identifiy what version of a particular application or service is running on that port.
- `-O: OS Scan`, this will send additional probes in order to determine what operating system the host is likely running.

Probing (`-P<x>`)

There are so many different options when it comes to probing a service however here are some of the specifics when it comes to probing things.

- `-Pn`: Don't ping the host, assume it's up - this is useful for hosts that don't respond to or block ping requests.
- `-PB`: Default probing, scan port 80,443 and send an ICMP to the target.
- `-PE`: Use a default ICMP echo request to probe a target
- `-PP`: Use an ICMP timestamp request
- `-PM`: Use an ICMP network request

Default Timing Options (`-Tx`)

Sometimes when tuning a scan you might want to have certain options set to speed up or slow down scanning depending on if you want to be noisy or stealthy!

- `-T5`: Insane; Very aggressive timing options, gotta go fast! This will likely crash unstable networks so shy away from it, in some instances it will also miss open ports due to the level of aggression.
- `-T4`: Aggressive; Assumes a stable network, may overwhelm some networks if not setup to cope.
- `-T3`: Normal; A dynamic timing mode which is based on how responsive the target is.
- `-T2`: Polite; Slows down to consume less bandwidth, runs roughly ten times slower than a normal scan.
- `-T1`: Sneaky; Quite slow, used to evade IDS and stay quiet on a network
- `-T0`: Paranoid; Very slow, used to evade IDS and stay almost silent on a network.

In addition to these options you can fine tune a scan even more with the particular settings most people use these options to speed nmap up, but they can also be useful for slowing Nmap down. Often people will do that to evade IDS systems, reduce network load, or even improve accuracy if network conditions are so bad that even nmap's conservative default is too aggressive., these flags are detailed in the following table:

Function	Flags
Size of the group of hosts to be scanned concurrently	`--min-hostgroup`, `--max-hostgroup`
Number of scanning probes to be launched in parallel	`--min-parallelism`, `--max-parallelism`
Timeout values for probes	`--min-rtt-timeout`, `--max-rtt-timeout`, `--initial-rtt-timeout`

Function	Flags
Maximum number of probe retransmissions allowed	`--max-retries`
Maximum time before giving up on an entire host	`--host-timeout`
Control the delay inserted between each probe against an individual host	`--scan-delay`, `--max-scan-delay`
Rate of probe packets sent per second	`--min-rate`, `--max-rate`
Defeat RST packet response rate by target hosts	`--defeat-rst-ratelimit`

Outputs

Viewing the output in realtime can be useful however parsing the information afterwards and feeding it into other tools is 10x more useful. Enter the different output options from nmap, saving to a file of one sort or another.

There's a few options to output to but mainly these are xml,gnmap & nmap and have the flags; `-oX`, `-oG`, `-oN` but there is also an easter egg output in 1337 speak which is `-oS`.

- `-oX`: This instructs nmap to give the output in XML format for parsing later.
    - Basic example: `nmap 10.0.0.1 -oX outFile`
- `-oG`: To do the same thing for a grepable file, `-oG` can be used. If I wanted to pull up the text from that file, I can use: grep `HTTPS` output.gnmap. This will search that file for the phrase `HTTPS` and output the result.

- Basic example: `nmap 10.0.0.1 -oG outFile`
- `-oN`: .nmap output will be the same as what is shown in realtime when you're running a scan, it allows you to quickly identify open ports or the bigger picture about a target.
  - Basic example: `nmap 10.0.0.1 -oN outFile`
- `-oS`: This option serves no real value over the past three however will output the results in a leet speak format for a bit of fun.
- `-oA`: Lastly to output to all the formats previously mentioned (.nmap, .gnmap, .xml) just give it a name and you're away.
  - Basic example: `nmap 10.0.0.1 -oA outFile`

Another useful output type is to view stats on the running scan. An example would be: nmap â€"stats-every 25s 10.0.0.1 to show me the statistical information every 25 seconds during a scan. You can use s for seconds, m for minutes, or h for hours for this scan. This can be done to reduce the amount of info filling up a screen.

Scanning a single host for top 1000 open ports

```
1  nmap -sT <host> --top-ports 1000 -oA TCP-Top-1k
```

This command essentially does the following:

- `nmap` : This is the name of the tool in use, nmap
- `-sT` : This flag tells nmap to do a full TCP Connect scan against the target.
- `<host>` : This is where the host goes either domain(blog.zsec.uk) or IP address(1.1.1.1)
- `--top-ports 1000` : This tells nmap to scan the top 1000 ports which are:

```
1,3-4,6-7,9,13,17,19-26,30,32-33,37,42-43,49,53,70,\
79-85,88-90,99-100,106,109-111,113,119,125,135,139,\
143-144,146,161,163,179,199,211-212,222,254-256,259\
,264,280,301,306,311,340,366,389,406-407,416-417,42\
5,427,443-445,458,464-465,481,497,500,512-515,524,5\
41,543-545,548,554-555,563,587,593,616-617,625,631,\
636,646,648,666-668,683,687,691,700,705,711,714,720\
,722,726,749,765,777,783,787,800-801,808,843,873,88\
0,888,898,900-903,911-912,981,987,990,992-993,995,9\
99-1002,1007,1009-1011,1021-1100,1102,1104-1108,111\
0-1114,1117,1119,1121-1124,1126,1130-1132,1137-1138\
,1141,1145,1147-1149,1151-1152,1154,1163-1166,1169,\
1174-1175,1183,1185-1187,1192,1198-1199,1201,1213,1\
216-1218,1233-1234,1236,1244,1247-1248,1259,1271-12\
72,1277,1287,1296,1300-1301,1309-1311,1322,1328,133\
4,1352,1417,1433-1434,1443,1455,1461,1494,1500-1501\
,1503,1521,1524,1533,1556,1580,1583,1594,1600,1641,\
1658,1666,1687-1688,1700,1717-1721,1723,1755,1761,1\
782-1783,1801,1805,1812,1839-1840,1862-1864,1875,19\
00,1914,1935,1947,1971-1972,1974,1984,1998-2010,201\
3,2020-2022,2030,2033-2035,2038,2040-2043,2045-2049\
,2065,2068,2099-2100,2103,2105-2107,2111,2119,2121,\
2126,2135,2144,2160-2161,2170,2179,2190-2191,2196,2\
200,2222,2251,2260,2288,2301,2323,2366,2381-2383,23\
93-2394,2399,2401,2492,2500,2522,2525,2557,2601-260\
2,2604-2605,2607-2608,2638,2701-2702,2710,2717-2718\
,2725,2800,2809,2811,2869,2875,2909-2910,2920,2967-\
2968,2998,3000-3001,3003,3005-3007,3011,3013,3017,3\
030-3031,3052,3071,3077,3128,3168,3211,3221,3260-32\
61,3268-3269,3283,3300-3301,3306,3322-3325,3333,335\
1,3367,3369-3372,3389-3390,3404,3476,3493,3517,3527\
,3546,3551,3580,3659,3689-3690,3703,3737,3766,3784,\
3800-3801,3809,3814,3826-3828,3851,3869,3871,3878,3\
```

```
34  880,3889,3905,3914,3918,3920,3945,3971,3986,3995,39\
35  98,4000-4006,4045,4111,4125-4126,4129,4224,4242,427\
36  9,4321,4343,4443-4446,4449,4550,4567,4662,4848,4899\
37  -4900,4998,5000-5004,5009,5030,5033,5050-5051,5054,\
38  5060-5061,5080,5087,5100-5102,5120,5190,5200,5214,5\
39  221-5222,5225-5226,5269,5280,5298,5357,5405,5414,54\
40  31-5432,5440,5500,5510,5544,5550,5555,5560,5566,563\
41  1,5633,5666,5678-5679,5718,5730,5800-5802,5810-5811\
42  ,5815,5822,5825,5850,5859,5862,5877,5900-5904,5906-\
43  5907,5910-5911,5915,5922,5925,5950,5952,5959-5963,5\
44  987-5989,5998-6007,6009,6025,6059,6100-6101,6106,61\
45  12,6123,6129,6156,6346,6389,6502,6510,6543,6547,656\
46  5-6567,6580,6646,6666-6669,6689,6692,6699,6779,6788\
47  -6789,6792,6839,6881,6901,6969,7000-7002,7004,7007,\
48  7019,7025,7070,7100,7103,7106,7200-7201,7402,7435,7\
49  443,7496,7512,7625,7627,7676,7741,7777-7778,7800,79\
50  11,7920-7921,7937-7938,7999-8002,8007-8011,8021-802\
51  2,8031,8042,8045,8080-8090,8093,8099-8100,8180-8181\
52  ,8192-8194,8200,8222,8254,8290-8292,8300,8333,8383,\
53  8400,8402,8443,8500,8600,8649,8651-8652,8654,8701,8\
54  800,8873,8888,8899,8994,9000-9003,9009-9011,9040,90\
55  50,9071,9080-9081,9090-9091,9099-9103,9110-9111,920\
56  0,9207,9220,9290,9415,9418,9485,9500,9502-9503,9535\
57  ,9575,9593-9595,9618,9666,9876-9878,9898,9900,9917,\
58  9929,9943-9944,9968,9998-10004,10009-10010,10012,10\
59  024-10025,10082,10180,10215,10243,10566,10616-10617\
60  ,10621,10626,10628-10629,10778,11110-11111,11967,12\
61  000,12174,12265,12345,13456,13722,13782-13783,14000\
62  ,14238,14441-14442,15000,15002-15004,15660,15742,16\
63  000-16001,16012,16016,16018,16080,16113,16992-16993\
64  ,17877,17988,18040,18101,18988,19101,19283,19315,19\
65  350,19780,19801,19842,20000,20005,20031,20221-20222\
66  ,20828,21571,22939,23502,24444,24800,25734-25735,26\
```

```
67  214,27000,27352-27353,27355-27356,27715,28201,30000\
68  ,30718,30951,31038,31337,32768-32785,33354,33899,34\
69  571-34573,35500,38292,40193,40911,41511,42510,44176\
70  ,44442-44443,44501,45100,48080,49152-49161,49163,49\
71  165,49167,49175-49176,49400,49999-50003,50006,50300\
72  ,50389,50500,50636,50800,51103,51493,52673,52822,52\
73  848,52869,54045,54328,55055-55056,55555,55600,56737\
74  -56738,57294,57797,58080,60020,60443,61532,61900,62\
75  078,63331,64623,64680,65000,65129,65389
```

if you're interested.

- `-oA` : Output the results to `.gnmap`, `.nmap` & `.xml`
- `TCP-Top-1k` : Name of output file

Some Options I Use

```
1  nmap -sSV -p- --min-parallelism 64 --min-hostgroup \
2  16 --max-hostgroup 64 --max-retries 3 -Pn -n -iL in\
3  put_hosts.txt -oA output --verson-all  --reason
```

The different flags in this command do the following:

- `-sSV`: This conducts a syn scan with version checks included.
- `-p-`: Tells nmap to scan all 65535 ports (1 - 65535), if you want to include port 0 you'll need to do `-p 0-65535`.
- `--min-parallelism 64`: Launch 64 parallel tasks to probe the target.
- `--min-hostgroup 16`: Scan a minimum of 16 hosts at one time and...
- `--max-hostgroup 64`: ... a maximum amount of 64 hosts.

- `--max-retries 3`: The amount of times to retry probing a port before moving onto the next service.
- `-Pn`: Skip ping scans, assume the host is up.
- `-n`: Skip dns resolution, usually select this when not interested in reverse dns or wanting a quicker scan :-).
- `-iL input_hosts.txt`: Take an input file containing target hosts.
- `-oA output`: Output the results to `.gnmap`, `.nmap` & `.xml` for parsing later and analysing.
- `--verson-all`: Do extended version checks against the host to find out services running.
- `--reason`: Detail the reason why a port is determined as open, filtered or closed.

Probing a specific service for more information and looking for known issues:

```
sudo nmap -sSV --version-all -p 11211 --min-paralle\
lism 64 --script=vuln 10.0.0.1 -Pn -n
```

The addition of the `--script=vuln` and specifc port tells nmap to only probe the port `11211` and tell me any vulnerable services it knows about running on that port. Additionally `-sC` can be used to scan a target and probe with common scripts. More information on the scripting engine can be found below.

One final one-liner I use a lot is to get the output of a subnet mask, something like:

```
nmap -sL -n 10.10.10.1/24 | grep report | cut -d " \
" -f 5 >> ips.txt
```

This will simply print all of the hosts in the range given as individual IP addresses, very useful when you don't have a subnet calc on hand or want unique ips for other tools!

Going Further

So going beyond normal scans, nmap does a lot more. It is capable of scanning IPv6 networks, has an inbuilt vulnerability scanning engine and can even be tuned to evade filtering. The next few subsections explain the different flags and features that can be leveraged to do these things.

Scanning IPv6

I've covered scanning IPv6 before in my post about pwning ipv6 things which you can read here[65]. However as a quick input the -6 or --ipv6 flags will instruct nmap that you're scanning an IPv6 address. Typically using something like:

```
1  sudo nmap -6 -sSV -p- -iL targets.txt -oA example_I\
2  Pv6 --version-all --max-retries 3 -T4 -Pn -n --reas\
3  on --vvv
```

Will work no problem, the breakdown of this command is as follows:

- -6: tells nmap that the targets are IPv6 hosts
- -sSV: instructs nmap to carry out a syn half-open scan & a version scan
- -p-: notes to scan all 65535 ports
- -iL: This flag tells nmap to load targets from a file path, loads from the current folder.
- -oA: notes the output to be in all three formats that nmap supports; XML, nmap & greppable nmap output.

---

[65]https://blog.zsec.uk/ipv6-pwn/

- `--version-all`: Sends additional version probes to attempt to discover the version of software running on each open port.
- `--max-retries`: Notes the maximum amount of retries nmap will do per port
- `-T4`: Adds additional timing options to nmap tuning the parallel processes and other timeout settings
- `-Pn`: Instructs nmap to assume the host is up and not to send ICMP packets to the target.
- `-n`: Tells nmap not to carry out DNS resolution of targets.
- `--reason`: Tells nmap to show the reason why a port is determined as open or closed based upon response.
- `-vvv`: This increases the verbosity of scan output.

Of course, you must use IPv6 syntax if you specify an address rather than a hostname. An address might look like 3ffe:7501:4819:2000:210:f3ff:fe03:14d0, so hostnames are recommended.

NSE - Nmap Scripting Engine

Most people reading this will have heard of metasploit framework(MSF), however a few may not realise that nmap has it's own vuln scanning ability built in. It's not a replacement for MSF but it has got some great features.

The NSE is a framework that runs code written in the programming language Lua with specific flags that the engine can parse. Lua is a lightweight, fast, and interpreted programming language.

I could write a whole article on its own covering the NSE side of nmap as it is so vast and includes many different options. Here are a few basic ones to get you started:

- `-sC`: This flag performs a script scan using the default set of scripts. It is equivalent to –script=default.
- `--script=vuln`: This will run a select set of scripts looking for vulnerable software, read[66] through the scripts it will run before running against a target to prevent unwanted outages.
- `--script=safe`: This will instruct nmap to only run scripts it deems safe against the target, these are bundled together with the intention of information gathering rather than exploiting issues.

A full list of the main NSE scripts built into nmap can be found on the nmap site here[67].

Evading Filtering

Here are some options that you might not know about that will help you in evading firewall blockages;

- `-sA`: TCP ACK Scan, this can be leveraged to find out if there is a firewall in place based on the response. It is always a good idea to send ACK packets rather than the SYN because if there is any active firewall working on the remote system then the firewall cannot create a log, since firewalls treat ACK packet as the response of the SYN packet.
- `-f`: This option tells nmap to use fragmentation and the scan will use tiny fragmented IP packets. The idea behind this is to split up the TCP header over several packets to make it harder for packet filters, intrusion detection systems, and other annoyances to detect what you are

---
[66]https://nmap.org/nsedoc/categories/vuln.html
[67]https://nmap.org/nsedoc/index.html

doing. This is all find and well but be careful with this, as some programs have trouble handling these tiny packets and could cause an impact on the application or service.
- `--mtu 24` : This flag can be used to set a specific MTU (Maximum Transmission Unit) to the packet. This is similar to packet fragmentation explained above. In the example given I have used the number 24 so the nmap will create 24-byte packets causing a confusion to the firewall. Bear in mind that the MTU number must be a multiple of 8 (8,16,24,32 etc).
- `-D RND:10`: This flag indicates the random number of decoy packets to send with each request, in an attempt to bypass network filtering or firewalls. You can instruct Nmap to spoof packets from other hosts. In the firewall logs it will be not only our IP address but also and the IP addresses of the decoys so it will be much harder to determine which system initiated the scanning. There are two options that you can use in this type of scan:

```
nmap -D RND:10 10.0.0.1 (Generates a random number \
  of decoys)
nmap -D decoy1,decoy2,decoy3 etc. (Manually specify\
  the IP addresses of the decoys)
```

It's also worth noting that the hosts being used as decoys must be online in order this technique to work. Also using many decoys can cause network congestion.

- `--source-port 80`: One surprisingly common misconfiguration is to trust traffic based only on the source port number. This flag can be used to change source port to throw off the scent of scanning. Simply provide a port number, and Nmap will send packets from that port where possible. Nmap must use different port numbers for certain OS detection tests to work properly. Most TCP scans, including SYN scan, support the option completely, as does UDP scan.

- --data-length 1337: Append Random Data to Packet for systems that use traffic shaping and other deep analysis.
- --spoof-mac Dell/Apple/3Com: This flag can be used to spoof the mac address of your scanning machine, this can be useful to bypass network access control that is based on the mac address of systems connected into the network.

There are of course more options that can be leveraged to evade and bypass IDS/IPS/Firewalls however the above should be a good starter.

Other Tooling with NMAP

Port scanning is great but nmap also has a suite of other tools that can be used, here's a quick overview on how to use them and some common options to try.

- ncat: Ncat is a re-invented version of netcat, it offers many more features over the standard netcat. It leverages both TCP and UDP for communication and was designed to be a reliable back-end tool to instantly provide network connectivity to other applications and users. It also works with both IPv4 and IPv6. In addition to this it also offers SSL support and proxying.
- ndiff: Ndiff is a tool to carry out a comparison of Nmap scans. It takes two nmap xml output files and shows the differences between them.

- nping: Nping is used for network packet generation, response analysis and response time measurement. It can generate raw network packets for various protocols. While Nping can be used as a simple ping utility to detect active hosts, it can also be used as a raw packet generator for network stack stress testing, ARP poisoning, Denial of Service attacks, route tracing and many more!

Nmap isn't the only tool for port scanning though, there are a few other great tools. The list below isn't a complete list of all other port scanners however is a collection of the few I use regularly. You may well encounter more throughout your learning journey.

- masscan
- metasploit auxiliary modules
- unicornscan
- netcat (to an extent)

Each of the tools above can be used for port scanning and they work in similar ways to nmap. Each has its "peaks and troughs" - PwnDexter[68], serving out different purposes and scratching different itches.

Masscan

Masscan[69] for example outplays nmap when it comes to huge IP address ranges and domain lists needing to be scanned. It is the fastest port scanner available as stated on its page; It can scan the entire Internet in under 6 minutes, transmitting 10 million packets per second!

---
[68] https://twitter.com/PwnDexter
[69] https://github.com/robertdavidgraham/masscan

Metasploit Auxiliary Modules

Metasploit[70] is a fantastic example of a fully fledged framework (try saying that quickly aloud!). It has many modules that fall under the auxiliary category each of which serves a different purpose and system. In particular, the scanner modules enable scanning of different systems and services in order to identify potential vulnerabilities. This list[71] on metasploit unleashed[72] outlines the vast amount of auxiliary modules available.

Unicorn Scan

Unicornscan[73] (first of all what a great name), is another port scanning tool very similar to nmap with varied output. It was designed to assist with information gathering and scanning using probing techniques to identify open ports. The main one-up it has over nmap is that it provides a more reliable UDP scanning engine allowing for discovery of open UDP ports.

Netcat

Netcat[74] isn't specifically a port scanner however it can be used to scan for open ports. It can be very useful when you compromise a machine and only have access to netcat. In order to port scan with netcat, the following line of code can be used:

---

[70] https://www.metasploit.com
[71] https://www.offensive-security.com/metasploit-unleashed/auxiliary-module-reference/
[72] https://www.offensive-security.com/metasploit-unleashed/
[73] http://sectools.org/tool/unicornscan/
[74] https://www.sans.org/security-resources/sec560/netcat_cheat_sheet_v1.pdf

---

Follow me on Twitter https://twitter.com/ZephrFish

```
1  nc -zv domain.com 1-1024
```

This will carry out a scan of ports 1-1024, it is obviously not as optimised as nmap but it does work!

Exploitation

Once you find open ports and have identified what services are running on those ports then next stage in this methodology is exploitation! This is the fun part where it rains shells hopefully. Now starting out you might have an output from nmap and not know what do do with it? Try grabbing the .nmap file and open it with nano.

```
nano results.nmap
```

Here's an example output of nmap, this was from a scan of all ports on one of the metasploitable[75] virtual machines:

Nmap scan report for 192.168.99.131 Host is up (0.00028s latency). Not shown: 65506 closed ports PORT STATE SERVICE 21/tcp open ftp 22/tcp open ssh 23/tcp open telnet 25/tcp open smtp 53/tcp open domain 80/tcp open http 111/tcp open rpcbind 139/tcp open netbios-ssn 445/tcp open microsoft-ds 512/tcp open exec 513/tcp open login 514/tcp open shell 1099/tcp open rmiregistry 1524/tcp open ingreslock 2049/tcp open nfs 2121/tcp open ccproxy-ftp 3306/tcp open mysql 3632/tcp open distccd 5432/tcp open postgresql 5900/tcp open vnc 6000/tcp open X11 6667/tcp open irc 6697/tcp open unknown 8009/tcp open ajp13 8180/tcp open unknown 8787/tcp open unknown 39292/tcp open unknown 43729/tcp open unknown 44813/tcp open unknown 55852/tcp open unknown MAC Address: 00:0C:29:9A:52:C1 (VMware) {/aside}

---

[75]https://information.rapid7.com/metasploitable-download.html

---

Follow me on Twitter https://twitter.com/ZephrFish

Look at all those open ports! Now some of you might already see a lot of juicy services running on this box that might gain you a level up pretty quickly. For those who've never seen the output from nmap in their life the basics are it is showing each port that is open, whether it's TCP or UDP and the service that nmap thinks is running on it.

I'm not going to step through each and every service however if you're interested in what each one does try googling it and have a read of each for extra learning. Instead here's a select few that would be fun to compromise and gain interesting information about:

PORT STATE SERVICE 21/tcp open ftp 22/tcp open ssh 23/tcp open telnet 80/tcp open http 111/tcp open rpcbind 139/tcp open netbios-ssn 445/tcp open microsoft-ds 512/tcp open exec 513/tcp open login 514/tcp open shell {/aside}

I've picked the services above mainly due to the nature of them being used to access the box remotely in some way or another. Be this to access files, in the example of ftp, telnet, NetBIOS, login & microsoft-ds or to login to a shell; ssh, telnet, exec, login, shell.

Each service presents a different way in. The basic output doesn't show any version numbers unfortunately. To better understand I'll run `-V --version-all`. This reveals that all of the services are severely outdated and likely running vulnerable software. The first port of call for me would be to try weak credentials against the services such as `admin:admin`, `test:test` & `user:user` against each service to see what will give up access.

If this doesn't work, then other exploitation techniques can be looked at such as using a framework such as metasploit to utilize other exploits. Simply launching `msfconsole` within

Kali Linux will launch the metasploit console which can be searched for exploits and modules relevant to the running services in your nmap output. Then each can be run against the target if you think the service matches up to the module.

If all else fails you could try an exploit from exploit-db[76] however be warned if doing this against anything live, **ALWAYS** run in a test environment first as exploits are like playing with fire! Especially running random scripts from the Internet always treat things with caution please. If you're using Kali Linux offensive security have helpfully included an offline version of exploit-db which can be searched using the `searchsploit` command.

There is a full write-up on how to gain access to metasploitable if anyone is interested is available here[77].

Pivoting/Further Recon/Post-Exploitation

All going well you've made it onto the machine you've been attacking and you have a shell! Well what's next? Well the answer to that question really varies and depends on a lot of things, mainly what is the scope of the engagement? Do you have permission to further traverse the network? Or is this in a lab environment?

If all is good, you have permission to proceed & want to gain more info about the system the first port of call would be to identify what privileges you are running with what your user is and what they can access.

---

[76]https://www.exploit-db.com
[77]https://community.rapid7.com/docs/DOC-1875

Information Gathering

So you find yourself on a machine, check your privs. To do this the first thing I'd do would be to view sudo if you can. To do this type the following command sudo -l if you have privs it will show something like:

```
1  $ sudo -l
2  Matching Defaults entries for apache on ltr101:
3      env_reset, mail_badpass, secure_path=/usr/local\
4  /sbin\:/usr/local/bin\:/usr/sbin\:/usr/bin\:/sbin\:\
5  /bin
6
7  User apache may run the following commands on ltr10\
8  1:
9      (ALL : ALL) ALL
```

If you see the above, you're pretty much golden! The user has FULL sudo privs and can escalate to root! Boom headshot do the root dance you're in!

...not so fast, in reality apache is hardly ever running as root and the user you land as in most situations might well be very limited. Try and find out what other users are on the system, there are a lot of different ways of doing this however the easiest would be to view the passwd file if available:

Follow me on Twitter https://twitter.com/ZephrFish

```
 1  cat /etc/passwd
 2  root:x:0:0:root:/root:/bin/bash
 3  daemon:x:1:1:daemon:/usr/sbin:/usr/sbin/nologin
 4  bin:x:2:2:bin:/bin:/usr/sbin/nologin
 5  sys:x:3:3:sys:/dev:/usr/sbin/nologin
 6  sync:x:4:65534:sync:/bin:/bin/sync
 7  games:x:5:60:games:/usr/games:/usr/sbin/nologin
 8  man:x:6:12:man:/var/cache/man:/usr/sbin/nologin
 9  lp:x:7:7:lp:/var/spool/lpd:/usr/sbin/nologin
10  mail:x:8:8:mail:/var/mail:/usr/sbin/nologin
11  news:x:9:9:news:/var/spool/news:/usr/sbin/nologin
12  uucp:x:10:10:uucp:/var/spool/uucp:/usr/sbin/nologin
13  proxy:x:13:13:proxy:/bin:/usr/sbin/nologin
14  www-data:x:33:33:www-data:/var/www:/usr/sbin/nologin
15  backup:x:34:34:backup:/var/backups:/usr/sbin/nologin
16  list:x:38:38:Mailing List Manager:/var/list:/usr/sb\
17  in/nologin
18  irc:x:39:39:ircd:/var/run/ircd:/usr/sbin/nologin
19  gnats:x:41:41:Gnats Bug-Reporting System (admin):/v\
20  ar/lib/gnats:/usr/sbin/nologin
21  nobody:x:65534:65534:nobody:/nonexistent:/usr/sbin/\
22  nologin
23  systemd-timesync:x:100:103:systemd Time Synchroniza\
24  tion,,,:/run/systemd:/bin/false
25  systemd-network:x:101:104:systemd Network Managemen\
26  t,,,:/run/systemd/netif:/bin/false
27  systemd-resolve:x:102:105:systemd Resolver,,,:/run/\
28  systemd/resolve:/bin/false
29  systemd-bus-proxy:x:103:106:systemd Bus Proxy,,,:/r\
30  un/systemd:/bin/false
31  Debian-exim:x:104:109::/var/spool/exim4:/bin/false
32  messagebus:x:105:110::/var/run/dbus:/bin/false
33  statd:x:106:65534::/var/lib/nfs:/bin/false
```

```
34   sshd:x:107:65534::/var/run/sshd:/usr/sbin/nologin
35   apache:x:108:65534::/nonexistent:/bin/false
36   user:x:1001:1001:,,,:/home/steam:/bin/bash
```

From this output we can see that there is another user on the system with shell privileges other than root, which is the user named user. To explain the passwd file some more here is a rundown of what each field means.

Taking the username user in this example, the first section signifies the username, the next section over separated by thr : character is an x which indicates that encrypted password is stored in /etc/shadow file. 1001 in the next two sections indicate the user(UID) & group(GID) IDs of the user; Each user will be assigned a user ID(UID) upon creation, UID 0 is reserved for root, 1-99 are reserved for other predefined accounts.

Further UID 100-999 are reserved by system for administrative and system accounts/groups. Anything 1000 and above signifies a normal user. The GID number code is the same as UID in the sense that 0-999 are reserved for different system accounts & anything 1000+ is a normal group. If a user has UID 0 and is not root this means that when they login they have root privelages.

The next section across (block 5 if you're counting), is a comment field to describe the user. Notice the list user has a desription of Mailing List Manager whereas the user has no comment which is replaced by three (3) commas. The last two sections; 6 & 7 indicate the home directory of the user & the command shell type.

Now to continue looking into escalation techniques I highly

recommend reading these two fantastic guides: g0tm1lk[78] & InfoSecPS[79] both focus on escalating your privs, Paul's article focuses on a combo of both which stands you in good stead.

Network Mapping

Once you're root or if you have enough privs to run things on the box, the next stage is to map out your surroundings. Is this machine on a network with a flat structure? Can you see other machines? My answer to that is ARP & netdiscover, both are very useful for identifying other machines on the network.

ARP is used to map MAC addresses (the physical address of the machine) to IP addresses on an internal network. Routers and switches send out broadcast ARP requests to all the MAC addresses on the network asking them to respond with their IP addresses. Each system will then respond with their IP address and the switch or other device will then create a small database that maps the MAC to the IP address, so that it it knows what machine is what and who is who. We as attackers or testers on a network can leverage this to identify other machines. An example on a Linux machine would be:

arp -a
? (192.168.1.67) at 10:ae:60:a4:3e:f3 on en0 ifscope [ethernet] ? (192.168.1.89) at 0:17:88:2e:76:48 on en0 ifscope [ethernet] bthomehub.home (192.168.1.254) at 5c:7d:5e:ea:c8:f0 on en0 ifscope [ethernet] ? (192.168.1.255) at ff:ff:ff:ff:ff:ff on en0 ifscope [ethernet] ? (224.0.0.251) at 1:0:5e:0:0:fb on en0 ifscope permanent [ethernet] ? (239.255.255.250) at 1:0:5e:7f:ff:fa on en0 ifscope permanent [ethernet] {/aside}

---

[78]https://blog.g0tmi1k.com/2011/08/basic-linux-privilege-escalation/
[79]https://infosecps.com/2017/04/22/privilege-escalation/

This shows all of the machines that respond to ARP requests on the local network which also discloses their internal IP address which we can try the scanning & enumeration phases against again. Alongside ARP there is also netdiscover[80] which uses arp to identify hosts but presents them in an easier to read format. The syntax for this command is as follows:

```
netdiscover -i eth0
```

Which will display hosts identified on the network. Additional to discovery, the scanning and exploitation phases can be carried out from the compromised machine by uploading pre-compiled versions of tools the the compromised machine or checking for an install of nmap or similar. Additional techniques that can be used includes port forwarding and proxy chaining. If you want to learn more about these techniques I highly recommend checking out the OSCP certification[81] from Offensive Security, it is well worth the cost for the training alone and the lab access which will allow you to try out your skills and learn new ones.

Pivoting

If you manage to exploit another machine on the network via your already established shell, you can start to pivot by utilizing some of the techniques mentioned above such as port forwarding and proxy chaining. Once you're on another machine other more malicious tools such as responder[82] can

---
[80]https://github.com/alexxy/netdiscover
[81]https://www.offensive-security.com/information-security-certifications/oscp-offensive-security-certified-professional/
[82]https://github.com/SpiderLabs/Responder

be used to gather user hashes and info on a windows domain with the goal of achieving domain administrator which is essentially Super-Admin! Additional to the manual enumeration and exploitation, metasploit also has a massive collection of post exploitation modules which can be leveraged to learn more about the target machine/network.

Other Types of Infrastructure Testing

Pwning IPv6

IPv6 is the demon that many testers dare not touch very often as it is still not the norm or widely adopted. Don't get me wrong, it is available(it has been for a while now). And, many big and small companies are using it but it isn't what a lot of people are used to & for this reason, there's not often much written down about how to hack at it, find flaws and exploit them. For this reason, this section will dive into what IPv6 is, some information about different schemas within the protocol & how to attack IPv6 addresses. Someone said to me recently to be able to hack something you must first understand the technology or app you're hacking. By this methodology, it is somewhat correct however I find myself and others winging it from time to time on obscure technologies!

A little bit of Background on IPv6

So for those of you who don't know, IPv6 is at some point going to be a reality for the content we all access on the internet. It created after one bright spark pointed out that the current Internet addressing system, IPv4, only has room for about 4 billion addresses.

Now that is a big number, but it doesn't account for nearly as many people on the planet, and thus connected devices.

So IPv6 fixes this issue by bringing: `340 trillion trillion trillion IP addresse` unique addresses to the table which dwarfs the 4 billion by quite a few.

Interacting with IPv6

Much like IPv4 addresses, interacting with IPv6 can be done in a multitude of ways and there are special addresses similar to IPv4 that do different things. Firstly when it comes to browsing to a web application over IPv4, it is as simple as chucking the address into the URL bar, and your browser will take you to the respective site/application on that IP.

However, when it comes to IPv6, you need to add a set of brackets around an address for your browser to recognise it.

So, for example, browsing to `https://[2a00:1450:401b:803::2003]` will give you an error on google however if you try to browse to it without [&] your browser will not understand it.

IPv6 Special Addresses

Like IPv4, IPv6 has a few special addresses and ways of doing things that should be noted. IPv6 reserves certain headers for different types of addresses. Probably the best-known example of this is that link local unicast addresses always begin with FE80. Similarly, multicast addresses always begin with FF0x, where the x is a placeholder representing a number from 1 to 8. The following list shows a select amount of these special address types.

- Link-Local
- Loopback
- Unique-Local(ULA)

Link-Local Addresses

A link-local address is an IPv6 unicast address that can be automatically configured on any interface using the link-local prefix FE80::/10. All interfaces of IPv6 hosts require a link-local address. It is valid only for communications within the network segment (link) or the broadcast domain that the host is connected to.

Simply put, a link-local address is created from the MAC address of an interface and the prefix fe80::/10. So anytime you see an address with fe80 as the prefix you can assume this is likely a link-local address however with all things it is always worth double checking.

The process involves filling the address space with prefix bits from the leftmost bit of the most significant bit and filling the MAC address in EUI-64 format[83] into the least-significant bits. If any bits remain to be filled between the two parts, those are set to zero.

Luckily there are tools for creating link-local addresses, so you don't need to worry about them, address6[84] will take a mac address which it is supplied and convert this to a link-local address, an example run of this command would look similar to:

---

[83] https://kwallaceccie.mykajabi.com/blog/how-to-calculate-an-eui-64-address
[84] http://manpages.ubuntu.com/manpages/trusty/man8/thc-ipv6.8.html

---

Follow me on Twitter https://twitter.com/ZephrFish

```
1  root@kali:~# address6 74:d4:35:4e:39:c8
2  fe80::76d4:35ff:fe4e:39c8
```

The tool essentially takes the mac address and straight converts it as can be seen above. Additionally, address6 can be used to convert a local-link address back from IPv6 to a mac address like so:

```
1  root@kali:~# address6 fe80::76d4:35ff:fe4e:39c8
2  74:d4:35:4e:39:c8
```

This tool is part of THC-IPv6 which is discussed more further down this post.

Loopback Address

In IPv4, a designated address known as a loopback address points to the local machine. The loopback address for any IPv4-enabled device is 127.0.0.1/8 this is also referred to as localhost. Similarly, with IPv6 there is also a designated loopback address for IPv6:

```
0000:0000:0000:0000:0000:0000:0000:0001
```

Once all of the zeros have been suppressed, however, the IPv6 loopback address doesn't even look like a valid address. The loopback address is usually shown as ::1. So if you see ::1 you can safely assume this is for the local machine and won't be routable over the internet.

Unique-Local Address

A unique local address(ULA) is the IPv6 equivalent to IPv4 private addresses; the current IPv4 private address ranges are those shown in the list below. These are intended for use in a single organisation's internal network. As part of RFC 4193[85], the address block fc00::/7 is reserved for use in private IPv6 networks.

IPv4 Private Addresses

- 10.0.0.0/8 IP addresses: 10.0.0.0 – 10.255.255.255.
- 172.16.0.0/12 IP addresses: 172.16.0.0 – 172.31.255.255.
- 192.168.0.0/16 IP addresses: 192.168.0.0 – 192.168.255.255.

It is important to know the local addresses as you may come across them on an external test and find yourself unable to reach them.

Prefixes in the fd00::/8 range have similar properties as those of the IPv4 private address ranges:

- They are not allocated by an address registry and may be used in networks by anyone without outside involvement.
- They are not guaranteed to be globally unique.
- Reverse Domain Name System (DNS) entries (under ip6.arpa) for fd00::/8 ULAs cannot be delegated in the global DNS.

As fd00::/8 ULAs are not meant to be routed outside their administrative domain (site or organization), administrators of interconnecting networks normally do not need to worry about the uniqueness of ULA prefixes.

---

[85]https://tools.ietf.org/html/rfc4193

Windows still doesn't fully support IPv6...

It is a little bit ironic however as hard as Microsoft has been pushing IPv6 adoption, Windows does not fully support IPv6 in all the ways you might expect. As an example, in Windows, it is possible to include an IP address within a Universal Naming Convention (\127.0.0.1ADMIN$, for example). However, you can't do this with IPv6 addresses because when Windows sees a colon, it assumes you're referencing a drive letter.

To work around this issue, Microsoft has established a special domain for IPv6 address translation. If you want to include an IPv6 address within a Universal Naming Convention, you must replace the colons with dashes and append .ipv6.literal.net to the end of the address — for example, FE80-AB00—200D-617B.ipv6.literal.net.

Attacking IPv6

Now that we've learned a little bit about IPv6 addresses, here comes the fun bit... Attacking them. There are a few toolkits for testing and hacking away at IPv6, however, there is a lot of room for development and creation of tooling to deal with IPv6 still.

One of the main things any pentester will use at some point will be Linux and more specifically the norm would be to use Kali Linux[86] or a Debian[87] Variant. Luckily for us, Kali Rolling(2016-Present) comes preinstalled with an IPv6 toolkit for a lot of different attack scenarios.

The main tooling used for infrastructure assessments have IPv6 modules built into them to allow us as the tester to do

---
[86]https://www.kali.org/downloads/
[87]https://www.debian.org

more! The conventional nmap & Metasploit type tools will work with IPv6, they just need some tuning and have some special options specifically for IPv6.

THC-IPv6

The Hacker Choice's IPv6 Attack Toolkit[88], is a collection of tools designed for probing and testing IPv6. I'm not going to re-write the descriptions for each in this blog post, check out the page for detailed info on each. However, the list below is a few I'd recommend for day-to-day IPv6 testing/hacking/p-wning.

- **alive6** - Shows alive addresses in a given segment, useful for quickly identifying potential targets in range.
- **dnsrevenum6** - Performs reverse DNS lookups for IPv6 addresses, useful for if you've got an IP and you want to find the domain associated with it.
- **exploit6** - Performs various CVE exploits, however, **BE CAREFUL** some of the exploits are unstable and could crash the host...
- **firewall6** - Runs a lot of access control list(ACL) bypass attempts to check different implementations of firewalling & restrictions.
- **passive_discovery6** - Passively sniffs the network and dump all client's IPv6 addresses, very useful for internal infrastructure assessments for identifying potential IPv6 targets.
- **trace6** - An implementation of traceroute for IPv6 which runs a bit quicker than traceroute6.

---

[88] https://tools.kali.org/information-gathering/thc-ipv6

The above tools are a select few that I've found pretty useful in the limited IPv6 testing I've done. If you have more suggestions, please tweet them at me[89].

IPv6 Port Scanning

Traditionally when it comes to port scanning there is one tool which is king; nmap! Rest assured nmap works for IPv6, all of the flags you know and love for IPv4 will mostly work on IPv6. To be able to scan IPv6, you'll need to add -6 before your targets regardless if it's an individual address or a file containing a list of addresses. Typically using something like:

```
sudo nmap -6 -sSV -p- -iL targets.txt -oA example_I\
Pv6 --version-all --max-retries 3 -T4 -Pn -n --reas\
on -vvv
```

Will work no problem, the breakdown of this command is as follows:

- **nmap**: the command to run the program
- **-6**: tells nmap that the targets are IPv6 hosts
- **-sSV**: instructs nmap to carry out a syn half-open scan & a version scan
- **-p-**: notes to scan all 65535 ports
- **-iL**: This flag tells nmap to load targets from a file path, loads from the current folder.
- **-oA**: notes the output to be in all three formats that nmap supports; XML, nmap & greppable nmap output.
- **–version-all**: Sends additional version probes to attempt to discover the version of software running on each open port.

---
[89]https://twitter.com/ZephrFish

- **–max-retries**: Notes the maximum amount of retries nmap will do per port
- **-T4**: Adds additional timing options to nmap tuning the parallel processes and other timeout settings
- **-Pn**: Instructs nmap to assume the host is up and not to send ICMP packets to the target.
- **-n**: Tells nmap not to carry out DNS resolution of targets.
- **–reason**: Tells nmap to show the reason why a port is determined as open or closed based upon response.
- **-vvv**: This increases the verbosity of scan output.

On top of nmap, there are other great port scanning tools such as zmap, which has been modified to enable support for IPv6 scanning, the modified version can be found here[90]. The GitHub page for the modified version lists that it supports:

- ICMPv6 Echo Request
- IPv6 TCP SYN (any port)
- IPV6 UDP (any port and payload)

Metasploit Framework

As well as port scanning, tooling such as Metasploit Framework support attacks for IPv6. Currently, Metasploit features a handful of scanner modules for IPv6 discovery, and IPv6 enabled versions of its traditional payloads. A quick and easy way to locate the IPv6 modules is to run the command `search ipv6` from within the Metasploit Console.

The majority of modules at the time of writing are related to payloads specifically for communicating back to the attacker's machine. However, the nature of Metasploit is that this will likely change in the future.

---

[90]https://github.com/tumi8/zmap

OSINT

Not only can IPv6 be a good target from a scanning perspective there are also many tools out there that can leverage IPv6 addresses for reconnaissance & open source intelligence gathering. Shodan[91] is a great tool I often use to discover information about an organisation. There is a simple search term that can be appended to a Shodan search: `has_ipv6:1` to find live IPv6 hosts tied to a search term.

Potential Goldmine

The security stack of an IPv6 system is relatively less mature than that of an IPv4 counterpart. Meaning that there are some potential issues that will have been overlooked. What I've found previously is that sometimes a company will have locked down their servers' IPv4 address & interface but completely forgotten about IPv6. Meaning that the usual ports: 3389,3306,445 etc are rightfully not exposed to the internet on their IPv4 interface but are wide open on IPv6!

This is where port scanning and the rest comes into play allowing you to poke and prod at systems(that you have permission to look at) to find holes and bugs. Once you've found an app or anything else it's as simple as `http://[ipv6 address]:port/path` and away you go!

Build Reviews

The cool hacking of things at a network level also extends beyond the black box scenario. It lends a hand to white box testing too. What is this you might wonder? Well, a

---

[91] https://shodan.io

build review or configuration review (the terms are interchangeable) is usually an assessment carried out against a system where the consultant or tester has full administrative privileges.

They're not as boring as one might think; sure, many penetration testers hate them. Personally I find them a fantastic learning resource for understanding how OSes **really** work. The objective of a build review is to compare and understand the setup that a client has against a gold secured build, this may be as simple as checking the patch level and password policy through to full CIS benchmark[92] compliance assessments.

Going through this and reporting as you go will teach you a lot about the ins and outs of how an operating system works and where key files are stored, this can be super useful later on when you come to being inside a network as a result of breaching the perimeter and haven't seen the OS before, however if you've done a build review you can use the knowledge learned from that to better move around the machine and find out more information.

You don't need to be a penetration tester to carry out a build review however, you can setup a lab environment yourself and do a mini-build review to find out where passwords can be stored, how the OS processes different types of scripts and processes and many more. If this is something you might be interested in have a read up of CIS benchmarks[93], the PDFs are free to download and will show you some of the checks that some testers will carry out against systems when carrying out a build review sometimes.

---

[92]https://www.cisecurity.org/cis-benchmarks/
[93]https://www.cisecurity.org/cis-benchmarks/

Breaking Out

Another fun task that can fall under infrastructure testing is a break out or kiosk assessment. This involves exactly what it says on the tin, the objective is to break out of a locked down or kiosk environment to access the underlying operating system (usually windows). You're only really likely to come across this in pentesting as I have yet to see any bounty programs offer something like this.

Breaking Out

7. Web Application Testing

Introduction

Continuing the theme of learning the basics, this section takes the position of web app testing and how to use some tools. It also touches on some things to look for and some general tips & tricks. It will mainly cover off the general topic however this can be applied to both penetration testing and bug bounty hunting.

For most of the people reading this, this may well be your first time looking at web applications from a hacking perspective. To get started its worth explaining my opinion on what web app testing is and how it can aid application developers in making apps more secure. This area not only serves as an introduction to the basics it also aims to give a mini overall guide on how to approach, setup and test web apps.

What Defines a Web Application?

There are many aspects that fall into the category however this is just a high level description. As a basic outline, a web application is anything accessed via a web browser without needing additional interaction such as flash, java, Silverlight etc. This can be expanded to explain the likes of static sites, thick clients & web services.

Follow me on Twitter https://twitter.com/ZephrFish

What is Web Application Testing?

Now we have a rough outline as to what qualifies as a web application. It's time to explain(briefly) what I mean by testing when I refer to web application (web app) testing. To spin it lightly, web app testing is the art and methodology of working through an application with an intent of identifying misconfigurations, vulnerabilities and general bugs. At a high level it is essentially looking for ways to hack the application to make it do things it's not meant to!

Why Web Apps Vs Infrastructure?

Personally I don't mind either however I feel having the skill set to test and assess web applications will stand you in better stead to enter the industry than that of someone with just infrastructure experience. Of course it is important to have a backing of infrastructure skills as well however to just focus on infrastructure is limiting yourself to what you can look at and learn.

The main reason for this being that there are more and more apps today than there ever have been before and they just keep becoming more popular. Additionally, we use the internet in an even greater capacity these days than before, upon this platform there are many web applications & sites.

Tooling

It is now time to move onto the tooling. Noting that this is for testing and not specifically bug bounty hunting. The tooling and techniques are slightly different.

Follow me on Twitter https://twitter.com/ZephrFish

The art of web testing is made up of many different areas, the traditional thought process would point directly to web applications however this can vary on a very wide scale. The sub-headings below explain some of the tooling that can be used for each stage of testing.

Browsers

Generally, the most common browsers for pentesting are Firefox & Chrome as these tend to be the most widely used by <s>consumers</s> victims. Personally I tend to use Firefox for most applications and chrome for more heavy applications that require the use of Java, Silverlight or Flash(heathen!).

Both have a great selection of plugins and add-ons. These are a few I'd suggest you check out:

- FoxyProxy[94] {for chrome and Firefox}: Good for quickly switching local proxy if channelling traffic through a proxy such as Burp Suite[95] the interface is easy to use and easy to setup.
- Wappanalyzer[96] {for chrome and Firefox}: Very useful add-on for quickly identifying the technologies used by the application or any frameworks in user. Particularly useful for noticing when applications are using AngularJS or other frameworks at a glance.
- Firefox Developer Tools[97]: It's in the name, this is only for Firefox however Chrome's dev tools that are inbuilt and can be accessed by pressing F12 (or if you're reading this on one of those new macs, well you made a bad

---

[94] https://getfoxyproxy.org/downloads/#proxypanel
[95] https://portswigger.net/burp/
[96] https://wappalyzer.com/
[97] https://addons.mozilla.org/en-Gb/firefox/addon/web-developer/

decision). The dev tools on Firefox as an add-on are great as there are many options including show all the JavaScript or other files on a single page including what's being loaded and where.

- Hackbar[98]: Again another Firefox only tool, personally I don't use this as I feel it crowds too much of the screen and most of its functionality can be achieved by using a local proxy however felt I should include it anyway as I've seen a fair few folks using it.

There are many other add-ons and extensions out there however the four described above are the most commonly used. Additionally, there are specific browsers that have been created for testing specifically OWASP Mantra[99] is worth mentioning.

It is a fork of Firefox but with tonnes of plugins and add-ons built in. I have previously used it before for pentesting however have found that with time it's better to use only the plugins you really want/need rather than have a million and one options!

Proxies

Once you have a browser setup how you like it, usually the next natural step is to setup a proxy to intercept traffic, manipulate it and look at specifics within an app.

The industry standard for this job is generally burp suite, as mentioned above. It comes in two flavours, free and pro. The free version feeds the basic needs of most as, it acts

---

[98]https://addons.mozilla.org/en-Gb/firefox/addon/hackbar/?src=search
[99]http://www.getmantra.com/

as a transparent proxy allowing modification of traffic and manipulation of requests/data.

The pro version however holds its own too, if you're working professionally as a pentester you cannot go wrong with Burp. It is a tool that should be in every web application tester's arsenal.

The benefit of using a proxy over testing 'blind' is that you can trap any request, play with it then pass it on to the application. By doing this you will find that a lot of issues pop out straight away such as client side filtering that isn't honoured server side or hidden values that are submitted in POST requests that contain juicy information. The list is endless as to why its a great tool and a great piece of kit to have.

There are other options out there too though, OWASP ZAP[100] & Fiddler[101] are other options if burp isn't for you. Both of these are free!

My Setup

Given all the tools of the trade I personally have a somewhat common setup to most, I use several tools in my day to day testing.

Testing Browser

The browser I tend to gravitate towards is Firefox with `FoxyProxy`, `Wappanalyzer` and the dev tools configured. Configured with burp's certificate for pass-through.

---

[100]https://www.owasp.org/index.php/OWASP_Zed_Attack_Proxy_Project
[101]http://www.telerik.com/fiddler

Proxy Choice

Burp suite pro is my weapon of choice when it comes to pentesting & for bug bounties I'll generally use a combo of Burp & Fiddler.

Burp Suite Features & Usage

In this section I will discuss the different features of burp suite, how to use them and how they are useful. I will also discuss some advanced tips for the pro version. Also note that some of the tabs are only available in the pro version.

What is Burp Suite?

Burp Suite (burp[102]) is a web application testing tool designed by Portswigger[103]. Currently it is the industry standard for web application penetration testing. It is also widely used by many individuals who partake in bug bounty hunting. This post discusses a few key features of the suite and some interesting tips along the way.

Project Files

Only available in the pro version

Project files very useful as I mentioned earlier, they store all of the traffic sent in a session including both in scope and out of scope hosts which can be useful to view later.

Essentially think of a project file like a temporary save location for information stored in your burp session that can be

---

[102] https://portswigger.net/burp/
[103] https://portswigger.net/

loaded at a later date. They work along side being able to save your session to disk which is accessible from the burp menu in top left hand corner of the screen burp > save state.

Target Tab

The target tab is one of the most useful tools within burp as it holds the site map for target sites that you are testing. Within the target tab there are two sub tabs, the Scope tab and Site map. Specifically, the main information for an application that you are testing is held within the site-map tab.

Scope

It can be configured so that only targets that are within scope are displayed. To do this first you'll need to configure the sites within scope. Navigate to Target > Scope then Include in scope.

This option will allow you to either paste a URL from the address bar or add manually using the add button. Additionally, you can load a list of targets from a text file using the Load button, this can be very useful for adding in several hosts at a time.

Top tip for open scoped engagements, if a scope states that *.domain.com is within scope you can add this to burp's scope using: ^*\.domain\.com$.

This will add all potential sub-domains into scope, what this also means is should you identify other hosts while browsing the main target they will automatically be added to scope and displayed in the site-map.

Tuning Site-map

Besides displaying all of the hosts browsed to in a burp session the site map tab can be tuned to only view the hosts you have set that are within scope. This can be achieved by clicking on the bar just below Site map and selecting Show only in-scope items. This will allow you to only view targets you've set as in scope.

This menu area also allows you to tweak what is displayed, it can be useful to view only requests that have generated types of errors.

Spider

The spider tab can be used for discovering content on a site however I don't use if very often as it does generate masses of traffic. Additionally, it can cause issues with the target applications if not tuned correctly.

To use it correctly, I suggest you disable the auto-form submission and auto login 'features' to insure minimal traffic generation. Doing so will prevent burp from attempting to flood the target site with form submissions of Peter Weiner/Winter.

Scanner

Only available in the pro version

The scanner tab is very useful as it picks up on 'low hanging fruit' vulnerabilities within an application. However, like all of the other tools within the suite it can be tuned to work better. By default, the options for it are pretty good but with tuning it can be great!

Pairing Intruder with Scanner

Only available in the pro version

To tune the scanner there is a little known trick that will allow you to pinpoint scanning. This can be achieved by trapping a request that has parameters you want to scan then, right clicking on it and sending it to intruder.

Once the request is in intruder manually select the areas in which you want to scan then select `Actively scan insertion points`. This will send the scanner off against only the points in which you've selected instead of randomly scanning points in the app/target.

This can be very useful for pinpointing vulnerabilities in applications that would otherwise be missed potentially.

Repeater

The repeater tool is arguably the most useful and powerful section within the burp suite tool set. It allows requests to be passed to it and modified then resent to the server. During a test I will spend a lot of time in here playing with requests and modifying different parameters to see their responses.

Specifically, it has two main uses, the first of which allows free manipulation of requests. Allowing you to target specific parameters and functions within an application. The second while not a feature or possibly not the intended use, it can be used as a clipboard/archive or interesting requests for you to go back to look at.

Imagine you're looking at an application which shows signs of processing certain characters differently, you can right click and send this to repeater to look at later. Having the request in repeater will allow you to manipulate it at a later time.

Intruder

The intruder tool has many many functions, however in this post I am only going to discuss a few of these. Mainly it can be used for fuzzing, error checking & brute-forcing.

In order to utilise intruder, select an interesting request either from the proxy intercept or another you've previously saved in repeater. Right click and select `send to intruder`. When the request is within intruder select the positions tab to select your inputs.

The payload positions are up to you to set, however burp will auto-select what it thinks are parameters, you can clear this using the clear button, then select your own ones by selecting the parameter then choosing `add` §. There are four attack types available to use in intruder, the subsections below explain what each does.

Sniper

The sniper attack takes one wordlist as an input and iterates over each parameter, one at a time. If you have multiple insertion points, it will enumerate the first parameter with all the payloads from the wordlist supplied and move on to the next and so on. It is best used when you're wanting to fuzz either single or multiple parameters with the same wordlist.

Battering Ram

Like the sniper attack, the battering ram uses a single wordlist however it will iterate over multiple parameters with the same payload for all the parameters. This can be useful when you're looking at how different parameters react to certain payloads.

Pitchfork

The pitchfork attack type runs through multiple parameters at the same time using different payloads for each parameter. This takes a single or multiple wordlists but will iterate through the words in the list split across selected parameters. An example of this is shown:

```
1  1st request - id=wordlist1[1]&param2=wordlist2[1]
2  2nd request - id=wordlist1[2]&param2=wordlist2[2]
```

Cluster Bomb

The cluster bomb attack type will take multiple wordlists and is useful when you have multiple parameters. It will run through over multiple parameters by using all the possible combinations of payloads from the multiple wordlists. So if you have multiple parameters, it will enumerate over one of the parameters with all the payloads from its respective wordlist, while the other parameters have the first payload from their respective wordlists loaded.

This can be very useful for when you are brute-forcing logins or other parameters/forms requiring two or more inputs.

Brute Forcing Basic Authentication

A scenario where intruder can be very useful is when it comes to brute-forcing a HTTP basic authentication login mechanism. In order to do this, first you must issue a base request with any values as the username and password, send this to intruder. I've included an example below.

GET /admin HTTP/1.1 Host: localhost User-Agent: Firefox
Accept: text/html,application/xhtml+xml,application/xml;q=0.9,/;q=0.8
Accept-Language: en-GB,en;q=0.5 Connection: close Upgrade-
Insecure-Requests: 1 Authorization: Basic YWRtaW46YWRtaW4=
{/aside}

Notice the bottom header:

`Authorization: Basic YWRtaW46YWRtaW4=`

this is the login value of admin:admin in `base64`. In order to attack this, we're going to use some of burp's more advanced intruder settings.

Mainly the custom iterator function, which allows you to split payloads up by a certain character or set of characters of your choosing. In this example I'll be demonstrating a brute-force using a wordlist, which in other words is a dictionary attack as opposed to a pure brute-force attack.

Using a custom iterator allows you to generate your own custom payload string consisting from several substrings. For each substring you can specify what the separator is which is basically a suffix. The Intruder calls these substrings "positions".

Setting up the attack, the first thing to do is select the base64 string in the `Authorization: Basic` header and change the attack type to `sniper`. Next go to the `Payload` tab and select the `Custom iterator` option from `Payload type` menu.

Next select `position 1` from the `Position` menu and load your usernames list in this . Put a colon (:) in the Separator for `position 1` text box.

Then change the position to 2 then in position 2, load the values you want to use for password guessing, just as you did for position 1. After you've set your two positions you need to tell the Intruder to encode the payload string using Base64 encoding. To do this go to Payload processing section and click Add button. Select Payload encoding option and then Base64.

By default, burp intruder will URL encode select characters, I recommend that you remove the = symbol as it is used by base64 for padding and this can introduce issues later on.

When this is done simply select start attack, burp will now run through the usernames and passwords you've provided.

Decoder

As with all of the tools within burp suite, each has a useful function. The decoder tool is all in the name, it decodes a select type of character sets and encoding types:

- Plain Text
- URL Encoding
- HTML
- Base64
- ASCII Hex
- Hex
- Octal
- Binary
- Gzip

Each of which can also be encoded into using the decoder tool. This is particularly useful for when you encounter parameters and data within requests which is encoded. By default, burp will attempt to auto detect the encoding however you can manually select which type of encoding to decode as too. Decoder can also be used to take checksums of strings, using a variety of hashing functions, these are located in the hash drop-down menu.

Sequencer

The sequencer tool has many functions but its main use is for checking the entropy of tokens and cookies. It is accessible by sending requests to it that can then be replayed in the 100s or 1000s to check the randomness of created values. This can be very useful for testing the randomness of cookie or CSRF token generation, mainly a use when testing authentication and authorization but can also be used for testing UUID and GUID values too.

Comparer

Comparer is essentially a diff tool to allow you to check the differences between two or more requests either based upon the words or bytes. This is useful when an application reacts differently to certain characters or words being used, it can be useful to identify more information about injection type vulnerabilities. To use it simple right click on a request and select send to comparer, then select a second request and do the same. Then navigate to the comparer tab and your requests should be there now. Simply select bytes or words, this will show a comparison of the requests you've sent and highlight the differences.

Extender

Finally, the extender tab is where add-ons/plugins for burp are located. Housed within this tab is where extensions can be installed and added. Additionally, all information surrounding various environment files such as Jython and Jruby can be set within this tab. This allows for usage of other 3rd party extensions build by developers that have been approved by Portswigger. Also located within this tab is information surrounding all of the APIs that Burp suite uses, allowing you to write your own extension. For more information on creating an extension check out Portswigger's site here[104].

Inbuilt Documentation

If you want to learn more information about certain aspects of burp suite that you're unsure of. The application does have a very comprehensive inbuilt help function. This is located in the help tab in the top menu bar.

What is your Methodology?

For web app testing usually I start off cold with manual discovery to get a feel for the application. Then content semi-automated discovery using tools like dirb & nikto which are both built into kali. My methodology varies per app per application of testing be this pentesting or bounty hunting I have two separate mind-sets. Reason being that bounties tend to have a much greater scope than a pentest where on a test usually one or two URLs/Apps will be in scope. A bug bounty may have `*.domain.com` in scope meaning the methodology can be switched up, I'd usually go after DNS then look at ports, then use something like Eyewitness[105] to screencap each app running HTTP/HTTPS.

At the end of the day I generally tend to test applications based upon my previous experience in pentesting whilst every day is indeed a school day. Some things are genuinely just broken same old.

---
[104]https://portswigger.net/burp/extender/
[105]https://github.com/ChrisTruncer/EyeWitness

But...what about Automated Tooling though?

To cover off all bases in tooling it would be rude of me not to mention automated tools. I've been asked before what's the best scanner or what tool is best for this job? As a blanket term the advice I'd give to anyone is, learn how to do everything manually before you even think of looking at automated scanning and tooling. For the sole reasons of:

- Not helpful for newbies
- Can be counter productive
- Learn to Walk before you can sprint
- Can have Inaccurate Results
- Will produce False Positives

When you are a bit more accustomed to manual testing only then should you venture forth into the world of automation. In terms of recommendations for automated tools there aren't many *great* ones in my opinion. In pentesting there is *Nessus*(it's expensive!) which is good for some things but terrible and inaccurate for others. There is also burp pro's scanner which is getting better and better with every update which is nice to see, kudos to Portswigger[106] for developing a great tool.

Methodologies

I have tried my best to outline tools for each stage of methodology below and further reading for each. ***Adapted from***

---

[106]https://portswigger.net/

my blog[107] *post*, hat tip to MDSec[108] for producing the Web Application Hackers Handbook.

Recon Tooling

Utilize port scanning, don't just look for just the normal 80,443; run a port scan against all 65536 ports. You'll be surprised what can be running on random high ports. Common ones to look for re:Applications: 80,443,8080,8443,27201.

There will be other things running on ports, for all of these I suggest ncat[109] or netcat[110] OR you can roll your own tools, always recommend that! - Tools useful for this: - nmap[111] - masscan[112] - unicornscan[113] - Read the manual pages for all tools, they serve as gold dust for answering questions. - Map visible content - Click about the application, look at all avenues for where things can be clicked on, entered, or sent. - Tools to help: Firefox Developer Tools[114] - Go to Information>Display links. - Discover hidden & default content - Utilize shodan[115] for finding similar apps and endpoints - Highly recommended that you pay for an account, the benefits are tremendous and it's fairly inexpensive. - Utilize the waybackmachine[116] for finding forgotten endpoints - Map out the application looking for hidden directories, or forgotten things like /backup/ etc. - Tools: dirb[117] - Also downloadable

---

[107] https://blog.zsec.uk/ltr101-method-to-madness/
[108] https://www.mdsec.co.uk
[109] https://nmap.org/ncat/
[110] https://www.sans.org/security-resources/sec560/netcat_cheat_sheet_v1.pdf
[111] https://nmap.org/
[112] https://github.com/robertdavidgraham/masscan
[113] https://kalilinuxtutorials.com/unicornscan/
[114] https://addons.mozilla.org/en-Gb/firefox/addon/web-developer/
[115] https://account.shodan.io/register
[116] https://archive.org/web/
[117] https://github.com/seifreed/dirb

7. Web Application Testing

on most Linux distributions dirbuster-ng[118] - command line implementation of dirbuster - wfuzz[119],SecLists[120]. - Test for debug parameters & Dev parameters - RTFM - Read the manual for the application you are testing, does it have a dev mode? is there a `DEBUG=TRUE` flag that can be flipped to see more? - Identify data entry points - Look for where you can put data, is it an API? Is there a paywall or sign up ? Is it purely unauthenticated? - Identify the technologies used - Look for what the underlying tech is. useful tool for this is nmap again & for web apps specifically wappalyzer[121]. - Map the attack surface and application - Look at the application from a bad guy perspective, what does it do? what is the most valuable part? - Some applications will value things more than others, for example a premium website might be more concerned about users being able to bypass the pay wall than they are of say cross-site scripting. - Look at the application logic too, how is business conducted?

Access Control Testing

Authentication

The majority of this section is purely manual testing utilizing your common sense and eyes, does it look off? Should it be better? Point it out, tell your client if their password policy isn't up to scratch!

- Test password quality rules

---

[118]https://github.com/digination/dirbuster-ng.git
[119]https://github.com/xmendez/wfuzz
[120]https://github.com/danielmiessler/SecLists
[121]https://wappalyzer.com/

- Look at how secure the site wants its passwords to be, is there a minimum/maximum? is there any excluded characters - ',<, etc - this might suggest passwords aren't being hashed properly.
- Test for username enumeration
  - Do you get a different error if a user exists or not? Worth noting the application behaviour if a user exists does the error change if they don't?
- Test resilience to password guessing
  - Does the application lock out an account after x number of login attempts?
- Test password creation strength
  - Is there a minimum creation length? Is the policy ridiculous e.g. "must be between 4 and 8 characters **passwords are not case sensitive**" – should kick off alarm bells for most people!
- Test any account recovery function
  - Look at how an account can be recovered, are there methods in place to prevent an attacker changing the email without asking current user? Can the password be changed without knowing anything about the account? Can you recover to a different email address?
- Test any "remember me" function
  - Does the remember me function ever expire? Is there room for exploit-ability in cookies combined with other attacks?
- Test any impersonation function
  - Is it possible to pretend to be other users? Can session cookies be stolen and replayed? Does the application utilize anti-cross site request forgery[122]?

[122]https://www.owasp.org/index.php/Cross-Site_Request_Forgery_(CSRF)

- Test username uniqueness
    - Can you create a username or is it generated for you? Is it a number that can be incremented? Or is it something the user knows and isn't displayed on the application?
- Check for unsafe distribution of credentials
    - How are logins processed, are they sent over http? Are details sent in a POST request or are they included in the URL (this is bad if they are, especially passwords)?
- Test for fail-open conditions
    - Fail-open authentication is the situation when the user authentication fails but results in providing open access to authenticated and secure sections of the web application to the end user.
- Test any multi-stage mechanisms
    - Does the application utilize multi-steps, e.g. username -> click next -> password -> login, can this be bypassed by visiting complete page after username is entered?(similar to IDOR issues)
    - Session Management
    - How well are sessions handled, is there a randomness to the session cookie? Are sessions killed in a reasonable time or do they last forever? Does the app allow multiple logins from the same user (is this significant to the app?).
    - Test tokens for meaning - What do the cookies mean?!
- Test tokens for predictability
    - Are tokens generated predictable or do they provide a sufficiently random value, tools to help with this are Burp Suite's sequencer tool.

- Check for insecure transmission of tokens
    - This lies the same way as insecure transmission of credentials, are they sent over http? are they included in URL? Can they be accessed by JavaScript? Is this an Issue?
- Check for disclosure of tokens in logs
    - Are tokens cached in browser logs? Are they cached server side? Can you view this? Can you pollute logs by setting custom tokens?
- Check mapping of tokens to sessions
    - Is a token tied to a session, or can it be re-used across sessions?
- Check session termination
    - is there a time-out?
- Check for session fixation
    - Can an attacker hijack a user's session using the session token/cookie?
- Check for cross-site request forgery
    - Can authenticated actions be performed within the context of the application from other websites?
- Check cookie scope
    - Is the cookie scoped to the current domain or can it be stolen, what are the flags set> is it missing secure or http-only? This can be tested by trapping the request in burp and looking at the cookie.
- Understand the access control requirements
    - How do you authenticate to the application, could there be any flaws here?
- Test effectiveness of controls, using multiple accounts if possible
- Test for insecure access control methods (request parameters, Referrer header, etc)

Input Validation

- Fuzz all request parameters
    - Look at what you're dealing with, are parameters reflected? Is there a chance of open redirection[123]?
- Test for SQL injection[124]
    - Look at if a parameter is being handled as SQL, don't automate this off the bat as if you don't know what a statement is doing you could be doing DROP TABLES.
- Identify all reflected data
- Test for reflected cross site scripting (XSS)[125]
- Test for HTTP header injection[126]
- Test for arbitrary redirection[127]
- Test for stored attacks[128]
- Test for OS command injection[129]
- Test for path traversal[130]
- Test for JavaScript/HTML injection - similar to XSS
- Test for file inclusion - both local[131] and remote[132]
- Test for SMTP injection[133]
- Test for SOAP injection - can you inject SOAP envelopes, or get the application to respond to SOAP, this ties into XXE attacks too.

---

[123] https://zseano.com/tut/1.html
[124] https://www.owasp.org/index.php/SQL_Injection
[125] https://www.owasp.org/index.php/Testing_for_Reflected_Cross_site_scripting_(OTG-INPVAL-001)
[126] https://www.gracefulsecurity.com/http-header-injection/
[127] https://zseano.com/tut/1.html
[128] https://www.owasp.org/index.php/Cross-site_Scripting_(XSS)
[129] https://www.owasp.org/index.php/Testing_for_Command_Injection_(OTG-INPVAL-013)
[130] https://www.owasp.org/index.php/Path_traversal
[131] https://www.owasp.org/index.php/Testing_for_Local_File_Inclusion
[132] https://www.owasp.org/index.php/Testing_for_Remote_File_Inclusion
[133] https://www.owasp.org/index.php/Testing_for_IMAP/SMTP_Injection_(OTG-INPVAL-011)

- Test for LDAP injection[134] - not so common anymore but look for failure to sanitise input leading to possible information disclosure
- Test for XPath injection[135] - can you inject xml that is reflected back or causes the application to respond in a weird way?
- Test for template injection - does the application utilize a templating language that can enable you to achieve XSS or worse remote code execution?
    - There is a tool for this, automated template injection with tplmap[136]
- Test for XXE injection[137] - does the application respond to external entity injection?

Application/Business Logic

- Identify the logic attack surface
    - What does the application do, what is the most value, what would an attacker want to access?
- Test transmission of data via the client
    - Is there a desktop application or mobile application, does the transferral of information vary between this and the web application
- Test for reliance on client-side input validation
    - Does the application attempt to base its logic on the client side, for example do forms have a maximum length client side that can be edited with the browser that are simply accepted as true?
- Test any thick-client components (Java, ActiveX, Flash)

---

[134]https://www.owasp.org/index.php/LDAP_injection
[135]https://www.owasp.org/index.php/XPATH_Injection
[136]https://github.com/epinna/tplmap
[137]https://www.owasp.org/index.php/XML_External_Entity_(XXE)_Processing

- Does the application utilize something like Java, Flash, ActiveX or Silverlight? can you download the applet and reverse engineer it?
- Test multi-stage processes for logic flaws
    - Can you go from placing an order straight to delivery thus bypassing payment? or a similar process?
- Test handling of incomplete input
    - Can you pass the application dodgy input and does it process it as normal, this can point to other issues such as RCE & XSS.
- Test trust boundaries
    - What is a user trusted to do, can they access admin aspects of the app?
- Test transaction logic
- Can you pay ££0.00 for an item that should be ££1,000,000 etc?
- Test for Indirect object references(IDOR)
- Can you increment through items, users. uuids[138] or other sensitive info?

Application Infrastructure

- Test segregation in shared infrastructures/ virtual hosting environments
- Test segregation between ASP-hosted applications
- Test for web server vulnerabilities - this can be tied into port scanning and infrastructure assessments
- Default credentials
- Default content
- Dangerous HTTP methods
- Proxy functionality

---

[138] https://www.rohk.xyz/uber-uuid

Miscellaneous tests

- Check for DOM-based attacks - open redirection, cross site scripting, client side validation.
- Check for frame injection, frame busting (can still be an issue)
- Check for local privacy vulnerabilities
- Persistent cookies
- Weak cookie options
- Caching
- Sensitive data in URL parameters
- Follow up any information leakage
- Check for weak SSL ciphers
- HTTP Header analysis - look for lack of security headers such as:
    - Content Security Policy (CSP)
    - HTTP Strict Transport Security (HSTS)
    - X-XSS-Protection
    - X-Content-Type-Options
    - HTTP Public Key Pinning

Hopefully this has been an insight into what to look for and how it can be looked for. Your own methodology is up to you, it is your responsibility to test and then act/report on what you've found.

Note Taking and Session Tracking

One of the most important tasks to do alongside hacking & reporting is note taking and tracking your work. Why? you might ask, because you never know when a session is going to die or you might use a cool one-liner and want to go back to it.

Keeping concise notes of what you are working on is very useful as it will allow you to keep track of little bugs you find, as well as notes on reproducing big ones.

Note Taking

When taking notes, there are many tools available for the task and it depends on personal preference too. Two common tools used for this are Keepnote[139] & Microsoft OneNote[140], Keepnote is cross platform and works on Linux, Windows & MacOS whereas One note is only Windows & Mac.

Others also find it useful to take notes in a text editor of their choice, my personal choice is to use Notepad++[141] or Sublime text[142].

When taking notes, I find it useful to keep track of what I'm looking at by splitting the tasks up into sections. So if I find an interesting looking application or port I'll put a section down for that. An example sketchpad of my notes for an example host, in this case I have used my base domain of `zephr.fish`, the ports noted are purely for example purposes.

---

[139] http://keepnote.org
[140] https://www.onenote.com
[141] https://notepad-plus-plus.org
[142] https://www.sublimetext.com

```
 1   == Target ==
 2   https://zephr.fish
 3
 4   == Interesting Ports ==
 5   3306 - MySQL
 6   60893 - Memcache
 7   8080 - Possible Web application
 8   60001 - Possible Application or DB
 9
10   == Web Applications Running ==
11   8080 - Apache Tomcat
12   60001 - Adobe Coldfusion
13
14   == Possible Attacks ==
15   RCE - ColdFusion(zephr.fish:60001)
16   XXE - ColdFusion(zephr.fish:60001)
17   XSS - Main Domain(zephr.fish:80)
```

The example above shows the target URL I've set out, any interesting ports I've identified and potential exploits available for the technologies running on the box. These exploits/vulnerabilities are usually gathered from a lot of Google-ing.

Note taking is a useful skill for any profession, it can be useful for summarising text you've read. I often find it very useful to comment on books/blogs/tutorials I've read to keep them bookmarked for the days I need them.

Topping it off, it is also very useful in testing, when you find a cool vulnerability and want to write it up before you move on.

Session Tracking

Going hand in hand with note taking is session tracking. Which is essentially noting all the commands you use, the packets you send and the URLs you might visit.

Now that sounds like a lot of work doesn't it? It does however it can be easily automated using some great tooling and tweaks to your methods.

You might also be wondering why would I want to keep track of the packets I send? It can be useful for many reasons however the main one being when pentesting, a client environment may experience downtime or issues then turn to the testers at the time to either pass blame or ask for logs.

Now, if we've been tracking our packets we can easily sift through all of the traffic that was sent to the target to pinpoint if said issue was a result of testing or not.

However, on the other side packet tracking can be very useful to identify how a service reacts to different types of traffic, it can also help you keep track of what content websites reference over different protocols. To achieve this job there are two tools I'd recommend: tcpdump[143] & Wireshark[144].

Tcpdump is a command line tool for tracking different types of traffic, it provides the user with an output of both source, destination IP addresses and ports. It comes into its own when you are running a server with only SSH access and no GUI.

Whereas Wireshark is essentially a graphical wrapper for tcpdump it still has its benefits as you can load pcap files into it that have previously been captured and use its filters

---

[143] http://www.tcpdump.org/tcpdump_man.html
[144] https://www.wireshark.org/download.html

Follow me on Twitter https://twitter.com/ZephrFish

to pinpoint certain traffic and protocols. To give some exposure/stuff to play with on Wireshark, try the following:

To start Wireshark

- Open up Wireshark from the Programs menu/open a terminal and type `wireshark&` **Note: This will not work on a ssh only server, also if you do not have it installed it can be obtained from here**[145].
- Start monitoring the LAN interface "Capture -> Interfaces..."
- Select the "Start" button next to the LAN interface on your machine.
- **Actions**
- Open a terminal
- ping `www.google.com`
- Open a web browser http://www.google.com
- Identify an ICMP request / response pair in Wireshark. *Tip, you can filter for ICMP traffic in Wireshark by entering "icmp" (without quotes) into the "Filter:" text box.* Identify a TCP handshake in Wireshark. Tip, filter on "tcp".
- Identify a UDP request / response in Wireshark. Tip, filter on "dns".
- Identify some none TCP / UDP traffic. What are these packets used for?

Sometimes network traffic isn't everything you want to track, what about that cool one liner you used to grep, cut and sed all the info from that index.html? Or that nmap line that bagged you all the ports and services you needed to find bug x?

---
[145] https://www.wireshark.org

For this there are several cool things build into *unix that can be used. The first of which is script[146] straight out of the manual page it is described as: `script makes a typescript of everything displayed on your terminal.`

How is this useful exactly?

For both pentesting and hunting it can be used to give a print out of all commands run, similar to the use of tcpdump/wireshark in a pentesting sense as you can use it as evidence in a report or feedback to a client. Similarly, in a bug bounty report it can be useful to demonstrate the commands and steps taken to find a bug.

Simple Usage of `script`

1. To start logging a session simply type `script ltr101.sh` (ltr101.sh can be named anything, this is just what I'm using for this example).
2. Type as normal, when done type exit.

Example Script

```
$ script ltr101.sh
Script started, output file is ltr101.sh
$ cat index.html | cut -d ">" -f 2 | cut -d "=" -f \
2 | sed 's/\"//g' > wordlist.txt
$ exit
Script done, output file is ltr101.sh
```

Now that we have the file saved it can be viewed either in your favourite file editor or printed out to the terminal with cat.

---

[146]http://man7.org/linux/man-pages/man1/script.1.html

Another highly useful command (more a shortcut) that can be used in Unix based systems is ctrl+r. I find it really useful to search back through my bash history to use the same commands again or edit them slightly. You can press the up arrow to go through your history. However, it can take a while if you're like me and type a lot of commands. Instead, try ctrl+r.

To do this: first press Ctrl + r, then start typing the command or any part of the command that you are looking for. You'll see an autocomplete of a past command at your prompt. If you keep typing, you'll get more specific options appear. You can also press Ctrl + r again as many times as you want to, this goes back in your history to the previous matching command each time.

Once you see a command you need or want to used, you can either run it by pressing return, or start editing it by pressing arrows or other movement keys (depending on your key bindings setup). I find this a really useful trick for going back to a command I know I used recently, but which I can't remember or don't want to look up again. It is also very useful when using ssh, if you can't be bothered typing in ssh user@x.x.x.x -p xxxx.

Finally, on the topic of session tracking there is one other key to keep in mind, however this is only related to web application & mobile application testing. This is the fantastic feature of Burp Suite Pro - being able to save your session & being able to store everything in a project file. Why might this be useful?

Essentially a project file on burp stores all of the traffic that has been passed through it, whether this be in scope or not (your scope is set in the scope tab of target). It also allows adds a failsafe should java crash (FUU Java) or windows decides updates need installed NOW. Or in general just to have a running log of things that are happening in the browser/burp session.

8. Importance of Reporting

In this section we will discuss the importance of reporting and what it means to me to create a beautiful, reproducible and verbose report. This can be applied to both a pentest or a bounty report as they are the same scenario, just slightly different writing styles (bearing in mind this is my opinion on this topic!).

When writing any security report especially from a technical standpoint, whether this be bounties or pentesting it is super important to have reproducible steps (I learned this from studying forensics at University).

As, essentially you are outlining your findings to a target be this a client or a bounty program. Most of us will find it really easy to post a report stating I found x wrong with y in this location. However, what does this look like to the client?

Sure, you might have found an ultra cool vulnerability or an interesting way of bypassing security control z, take a second to think, the client might not see the same thing that you do. IN their mind they may be thinking: *"Interesting, but how the hell did you get there? What do I need to do to reproduce and fix it?"* HELP PLEASE!.

So an answer here to this is creation of a verbose report, one that has the necessary information contained within it to allow said client to not only reproduce what you found but also with detailed steps and references to correctly fix the issue.

The next few sections will explain the structure I follow to create a decent report, note this might not be what you are used to however you will thank me for it later when programs are singing your praises due to the detail of your report.

Reporting in Pentesting

A penetration test report is more often tailored to multiple reading groups and as a result needs to be broken down into multiple sections for easier digestion by the business. The typical readers tend to be C-Level executives, Technical managers, project managers, developers and IT folks.

In a nutshell, usually you don't want to be dropping acronyms left right and centre like XSS, CSRF, and other buzzwords to management. Usually (but not always) it will go over their head and disadvantage you in putting your point across. Instead consider writing like you are explaining the issue to your granny or a non technical friend "*#teachgranny*" - cornerpirate[147].

Consider phrases such as "This would enable a malicious attacker to gain access to user information which could result in loss of sensitive data" as an example. However, when pitching your point to the technical teams you can outline in more detail explaining what the issue is, who can exploit it and what the impact is of said bug.

The sections in a pentest report will usually contain (but are not limited to) headings such as:

---

[147] https://twitter.com/cornerpirate

1. Management/Executive Summary
2. Scope/Targets
3. Table of issues/recommendations
4. Vulnerabilities Discovered
5. Additional Information

Usually a pentest report will span over 50-60 pages at a minimum, however this can be any number realistically depending on an unlimited amount of variables.

Breaking down the reporting sections a bit; when writing, I personally write the above in reverse order. Starting with findings, then technical summary and finally executive summary. This is based on having completed the findings it is easier to then convert what was found to content that is easily digestible by a non-technical reader.

It is important to factor in the target audience and how much time they're likely to be able to spare to read the report, this is just as important for digesting your first pentest report as it is writing one!

If you are reading this as you have or are about to receive your first technical pentest report then the following subsections detail where each section is relevant to the business and how sections can be ingested.

- Chief Executive Officer(CEO)/Managing Director/Board Director: Usually have minimal time on their hands and as a result will probably not read beyond page 1. For this reason they will need a visual representation of findings to indicate the areas where they need to invest in, immediate risks to the business and any impact to operations of the business. Additionally they may need to summarise the findings and report back to their board, therefore concise findings that detail impact in the executive summary are important.

- Chief Technical Officer (CTO) - As this role is usually a bit more technically understanding they will probably get to page 3, they may skim read any critical vulnerabilities to get a feel for what level of effort is required and any graphical presentation of results. Their main priority is to know what action to take in the business and where: are there issues with developers (in house or outsourced), network team or hosting partners or network kit, how will this impact the business and do they need to ask for more budget from the CEO/CFO/Board?
- Chief Information Security Officer/Security Manager - In bigger organisations may not have time to read the entire report but will read the business and technical summaries, therefore the first two sections need to detail the impacts in a manner that is understandable and actionable. In smaller companies the CISO will likely read the entire report minus the tail end of lower risk vulnerabilities, they will need technical detail and remediation advice. Details of the overall trends observed during the engagement that will enable them to present results to the risk committee and executive board.
- Devops/Developers/IT Network folks i.e the front line techies - Will read the vulnerabilities and findings that they have been told to fix, the findings section for them will need clear details on how to reproduce, a recommendation and references that will enable them to deploy a fix for said issue.

Follow me on Twitter https://twitter.com/ZephrFish

Making Things Beautiful

Now we understand our target audience it is time to have a look at what each section might look like and what level of depth each should go into when writing the report. As I said above this is in reverse order and how I would approach it based on experience working with different consultancies each company will do it slightly different.

Making things beautiful in reporting is really easy, it depends on how you're representing your information though, whether this be within Microsoft Word, markdown or another format of your choice. The key point to understand is you want to portray your information in the clearest way possible.

Essentially when creating reports, the main thing is understanding your format, so if it's bug bounty reports you're after then you'll want to get a greater understanding of the formatting within markdown, how to outline your data in a pretty and readable form.

Stay Beautiful, Stay Verbose. Enjoy your work.

Enjoy reporting your issues and putting your point across in a clear manner.

Technical Findings

When you are describing your findings for the report there are key areas that should be included. Specifically there should be a short description of the issue identified explaining how it impacts the affected host/application/area then detailing how that is a risk to end users or interactions.

Findings should also include where possible evidence such as screenshots, photographs, output that can be read clearly outlining the issue or other documentation. As with all things when it comes to reporting every person and company will do it slightly different. However, the technique I learned back when I was doing a forensics degree and backed up by my mentor; Paul Ritchie was:

- Introduce
- Show
- Discuss

Introduce the finding, explain what the issue is where it is located and how to reproduce it, show evidence regarding the finding document multiple steps to reproduce in a clear manner to enable the client or another tester to reproduce the issue. More evidence is always better than less and providing steps that are understandable is key!

An example finding write up is shown below to allow you to better understand how to represent information, here is a write up of an exposed telnet management interface. It is purely fictional but gives an overview of what a finding may look like in a penetration testing report. The IP address used is 127.0.0.1 for illustration purposes and a false organisation called ZSEC Industries.

Description

Infrastructure testing identified that ZSEC Industries were exposing administrative management services. These services were not limited through strict access control and allowed anyone to connect and attempt to login. Administrative interfaces are a major target for external attackers as they may enable the attacker to gain full compromise of the application or the underlying infrastructure with a valid set of credentials.

It was found that the services included telnet and file transfer protocol(FTP) which transmit data in clear text between the client and server. It would therefore be possible for a suitably placed attacker to intercept the data and derive the credentials. Usually at an internet service provider level or on the same network if on the internal network, this especially becomes a problem when there is a flat network structure in place.

Of further concern, was that host did not require a username to be supplied to login. This increases the chances of a successful brute-force attack. The following output from the telnet command details a connection to the service:

```
1  root@testing:~/zsec$ telnet 127.0.0.1 9999
2  Trying 127.0.0.1...
3  Connected to 127.0.0.1.
4  Escape character is '^]'.
5  *** Lantronix UDS2100 Device Server ***
6  MAC address 00AABBCCCCEE
7  Software version V6.1.0.2 (060719)
8  Password :
```

The services were found to be vulnerable to brute force attacks. These attacks are common vectors against Internet exposed interfaces and a number of tools can be used to automate these activities. If an attacker could successfully obtain credentials through this method, they would have control of the application in the context of the compromised user.

The consultant was able to successfully brute-force access using a tool called hydra which carries out various brute-force attacks with a supplied wordlist:

```
hydra -P 500-worst-passwords.txt 127.0.0.1:9999 telnet
```

It was found that the password was within the 500 worst passwords list which granted the consultant administrative privileges on the device:

Authentication Successful admin@127.0.0.1 > whoami > admin {/aside}

The affected system was: - 127.0.0.1 - localhost - 9999/tcp

Recommendation

It is recommended that all management services utilise stricter access control to limit access to only those IP addresses or users that are required. Access control lists should be used to specify only specific source addresses, where possible. All management services, whether exposed or not should protect client communications through cryptographic technologies, included in protocols such as HTTPS and SSH.

Technical Summary

Once you've completed your findings write up it can be very useful to produce a technical summary. The aim of this is to give the reader a quick reference to the issues identified, what their risk rating is and an overview of how to remediate them. As mentioned in the target readers section this will be most likely read by technical C-level staff and technical managers, it may also be read by front line techie team leads who need to distribute sections of the report to their team.

Often this can be represented in a table or a few short paragraphs that dive into more technical detail than the management summary. The primary focus of this summary should be around highlighting the points of interest and requirements for remediation that can be understood by a technical audience.

An example technical summary built from the tech findings discussed above: The testing against ZSEC industries found that there was a large number of issues that affected the external infrastructure. During this period of testing, there were three (3) high-risk, one (1) medium-risk, and one (1) low risk vulnerabilities identified.

Management/Executive Summary

Once you've written out all of your findings in technical form, the next area to write is the management summary. The summary is generally going to be read by a non technical audience. I always refer back to a phrase that @CornerPirate coined; #TeachGranny. Take everything you're about to explain in the management summary and try to explain it in terms that your granny could understand.

The language in the summary should focus on the risks to the business, why should the reader care about the issues what quantifies them as an impact to their business? In essence the exec summary is usually split up like a story would be, with an introduction, a middle (this is where you explain the risks to the client's C level) and an end, usually consisting of a conclusive summary of the fixes required. An example executive summary is shown below;

ZSEC Industries(ZSEC) contracted with ZephrSec to perform a security assessment of their external infrastructure

estate. The engagement occurred during the period from 13/01/2020 and 19/01/2020. The objective of the engagement was to identify vulnerabilities in ZSEC's systems and network security that both internal and external adversaries could exploit.

During the assessment, there were three high risk issues identified, these were primarily found to affect administrative and business applications that were internet facing. An attacker could leverage the risks identified to gain access to network management interfaces which could enable them to access further systems on ZSEC's internal network. By doing so, an attacker would breach the confidentiality of information held on the system and this could have further impact on the integrity and availability of systems.

Testing has highlighted issues, mainly related to systems hardening and configuration issues; however, by remediating these issues, ZSEC will harden the security of their perimeter and underlying systems. By making some configuration changes, most of the issues identified can be resolved.

It is essential that patching processes are reviewed to ensure all servers and third party software remain updated. This process should be reviewed as patching mitigates the vulnerabilities present in older versions of the software. The recommendations found during this test should be reviewed and addressed based on the client's internal risk rating for each issue.

Important takeaways from the above summary is to write with confidence in your findings. Also provide advice that is actionable for the board or non-technical users, try to avoid acronyms where possible and overly verbose language.

Pulling it Altogether

Once you've written your report, you should have an executive summary, a technical summary, some findings and depending on those findings potential appendixes detailing more information on said findings. Most organisations will have a quality assurance (QA) process whereby the report is reviewed for any technical inaccuracies and grammatical errors.

Typically this is done by two separate people to account for any potential oversights and help tidy up the report for delivery so that the final product is error free and reads well.

Final Note on Pentest Reporting

Whether you're writing or receiving a report be it your first or five thousandth report, it is important to take care of each. If you are on the receiving end most times it should be pretty straight forward to digest each segment of the report and sufficiently segregate the sections between relevant teams in your organisation.

Bug Bounty Reporting

Similar to pentest reporting, bug bounty reporting is all about conveying what you have found in a reproducable manner with a decent recommendation that will enable developers to take your bug and apply a fix. One could argue that the same structure should be followed for pentesting but the addition to a pentest report being the executive & technical summary.

Normally when I find a bug on a program I will take the extra time to craft a unique report for the affected client and the affected area of the application or site. However usually I will follow this vague structure:

1. Issue Description
2. Issue Identified
3. Affected URL/Area
4. Risk Breakdown
5. Steps to Reproduce
6. Affected Demographic/User base
7. Recommended Fix or Remediation Steps
8. References
9. Screenshots of the issue to reproduce

To quickly explain what each of these headers should contain here's an outline:

- **Issue Description** - A generic overview of the issue, I usually use the default text from OWASP as it explains the issue well.
- **Issue Identified** - A more specific description of the issue identified within the application.
- **Affected URL/Area** - The affected URLs or area of the application where the issue exists.
- **Steps to reproduce** - A clear outline of the steps required to execute the payload as an attacker, this can include how to setup the payload and launch it.
- **Affected Demographic/User Base** - Explain who this issue affects? Is it everyone or just a select amount of users? How can this occur?

- **Recommended Fix** - How do you fix the issue? What is the recommended remediation actions required to successfully fix issue x? This is arguably the most important in conjunction with steps to reproduce as not only do you need to notify a program where an issue exists but also how to effectively fix it.
- **References** - Include additional reading for the client to further backup the issues explained or elaborate more on other potential issues chained to the one identified.

Now, not every report I deliver to a program is going to have this applicable structure as it obviously depends on the issue identified. Creation of a properly verbose and informative report can be dialled down to a methodology taught to me by the man who taught me to report properly when I first started out in testing (cornerpirate[148]): *Introduce, Show, Explain.*

Essentially you are presenting your evidence, showing how it's possible to do *X* then explaining how it's an issue or what it demonstrates.

To put this structure into context here is an example bug report that typically I might submit. This particular issue is an example of stored cross site scripting within a file upload feature. All of the information outlined in this example has been created for this blog post and isn't live data :-).

Issue Description

Cross-Site Scripting (XSS) attacks are a type of injection, in which malicious scripts are injected into otherwise benign and trusted web sites. XSS attacks occur when an attacker uses a web application to send malicious code, generally in the form of a browser side script, to a different end user.

---

[148]https://twitter.com/cornerpirate

Issue Identified

The consultant identified that the update profile picture is vulnerable to cross site scripting, it is possible to upload an image with a MIME type of text/html this is then stored on the user's profile as an XSS payload, the outline below demonstrates the steps taken to exploit and reproduce.

Risk Breakdown

- Risk: **High**
- Difficulty to Exploit: **Medium**

Affected URLs

- https://example.com/update-profile
- https://example.com/file/upload

Steps to Reproduce

The following steps indicate a proof of concept outlined in three (3) steps to reproduce and execute the issue.

Step 1: Navigate to https://example.com/update-profile and select edit as shown in screenshot attached labelled step1.jpg.

Step 2: Modify the profile image request with a local proxy, in this case the consultant is using Burp Suite. Change the Content type from image to text/html as shown in the post request:

```
1   POST /file/upload/ HTTP/1.1
2   Host: example.com
3   ---snip----
4
5   ---------------------------900627130554
6   Content-Disposition: form-data; name="stored_XSS.jp\
7   g"; filename="stored_XSS.jpg"
8   Content-Type: text/html
9
10  <script>alert('ZephrFish')</script>
11  ---------------------------900627130554
```

When this is sent, the following response is shown:

```
1   HTTP/1.1 200 OK
2   Date: Sat, 13 Aug 2016 14:31:44 GMT
3   ---snip---
4
5   {"url": "https://example.com/56fc3b9215900627130554\
6   3ef45a04452e8e45ce4/stored_XSS.jpg?Expires=14656699\
7   04&Signature=dNtl1PzWV&Key-Pair-Id=APKAJQWLJPIV25LB\
8   ZGAQ", "pk": "56fc3b92159006271305543ef45a04452e8e4\
9   5ce4/stored_XSS.jpg", "success": true}
```

Step 3: The file has been uploaded to Application X and is hyperlinked to from the profile page as shown in step 3.jpg. By simply following the link to the image which in this case is:

```
1       https://example.com/56fc3b92159006271305543ef45\
2   a04452e8e45ce4/stored_XSS.jpg
```

Follow me on Twitter https://twitter.com/ZephrFish

The payload is executed as shown in attached screenshot labelled step3.jpg, thus this demonstrates the issue is stored cross site scripting.

Affected Demographic

This issue will affect all users on the site who view the profile of the attacker, when the image is rendered the payload is executed instead of a profile image. Additionally, when the malicious user posts anything on the forums the payload will execute.

Remediation Instructions

Insure that file upload checks the MIME type of content being uploaded, for additional security implement server side content checking to ensure file headers match that of the file extension. Additionally, make sure that all user input is treated as dangerous do not render any HTML tags.

References

For more information on remediation steps check out reference [2][149].

- OWASP XSS Explained[150]
- OWASP XSS Prevention Cheat Sheet[151]

---

[149] https://www.owasp.org/index.php/Cross-site_Scripting_(XSS)
[150] https://www.owasp.org/index.php/Cross-site_Scripting_(XSS)
[151] https://www.owasp.org/index.php/XSS_(Cross_Site_Scripting)_Prevention_Cheat_Sheet

9. Social & People Skills

For most of you reading this series you might have seen the first few technical articles then one about reporting, now you're seeing this about people skills. It's got you thinking now hasn't it? Why do I need to talk to people irl[152]? I WANT TO HACK THE PLANET! Alright calm down there Dade[153].

Yes, having technical skills are great they're awesome in fact and really fun to learn. However, it is important if you want to actually become a pen-tester or a consultant you're going to need to talk to clients or other humans at some point.

There is a phrase I've heard many a time in the lead up to starting my career: *"It's not only what you know but it's who you know"*. And, this rings very true when it comes to starting out, you could have a top degree, some 31337 skills and/or be pwning things every day of the week. If you can't actually speak to another human in real life you're not going to get too far.

Fear not! There are great ways to gain contacts really easily and effectively. These skills come in two of many flavours, mainly meetups and conferences (there are other ways too but these will be what I talk about here).

---

[152]https://en.wikipedia.org/wiki/Real_Life
[153]https://en.wikipedia.org/wiki/Hackers_(film)

Meetups

In security and technology there are a mass multitude of meetups in most cities and you'd be surprised at how not well known these can be. They are usually a great way to meet local like minded individuals from many backgrounds who share the same interests as you.

Additionally, they may too share the social awkwardness factor, and this adds to the building of your people skills. Nobody is going to judge you for talking to people and if they do well they're only ruining their own potential connections.

An example of great meetups for hackers and security folks alike is local DEF CON and OWASP groups. In Glasgow[154] I run the local DEFCON Chapter DC44141[155] however there are many other groups if you're not in Glasgow. For DEFCON Chapters you can find a list of all official one on the DEFCON Website or by simply doing a quick google search.

Alternatively, there are also OWASP meetups[156] in many cities for those of you interested in web application security.

Don't let these two groups be your limit though, there is a vast multitude of other meetups in other cities all it takes is some googling and searching on twitter to find something you might like.

---
[154] https://www.meetup.com/Glasgow-Defcon-DC44141/events/233060708/
[155] https://twitter.com/DC44141
[156] https://www.meetup.com/find/events/?allMeetups=false&keywords=OWASP&radius=Infinity

Conferences

Much like meetups, conferences tend to be great for meeting and chatting to like minded folks as well. They have the added benefit usually of having interesting talks at them too related to a topic of interest.

As far as security conferences go there are a few key ones to check out both international and UK based. Below is a short list of my favourites, bearing in mind this is not a comprehensive list, there are others available and I would encourage you to seek them out.

UK Conferences

- BSides Manchester[157]
- Steelcon[158]
- BSides London[159]
- BSides Edinburgh[160]
- BSides Belfast[161]
- 44Con[162]
- Securi-Tay[163]

International Conferences

- DEF CON Las Vegas[164]

---

[157] http://www.bsidesmcr.org.uk/
[158] https://www.steelcon.info/
[159] https://www.securitybsides.org.uk/
[160] https://www.bsidesedinburgh.org.uk/
[161] https://bsidesbelfast.org/
[162] https://44con.com/
[163] https://securi-tay.co.uk/
[164] https://www.defcon.org/

Follow me on Twitter https://twitter.com/ZephrFish

- Hack in The Box[165]
- Appsec EU[166]
- BSides Athens[167]
- Blackhat USA[168]/Europe[169]

Having given a small list of things to checkout hopefully you'll make the effort and go to a meetup or conference. By doing so you will not only benefit yourself but you will help grow a great community. On top of going to conferences as an attendee, look at doing a talk if you fancy it!

Not only can you share a topic you enjoy but you can also increase your people skills by pushing the boat out that little bit further.

---

[165] http://www.hitb.org/
[166] http://2016.appsec.eu/
[167] http://www.bsidesath.gr/
[168] https://www.blackhat.com/
[169] https://www.blackhat.com/eu-16/

10. Penetration Testing, Bug Bounty Hunting & <Insert Colour Teaming>

This section will discuss the differences between choosing penetration testing as a career path vs doing bug bounties. It will also discuss the different teams that there are in security and enable you to better understand how the all fit together.

As many of you will know I have experience in pentesting, bounties, red team and purple teaming, while doing penetration testing as a day job I do enjoy partaking in bug bounty hunting in my free time. I find they pair nicely against each other lending new skills to each.

There is an ongoing discussion I'm seeing again and again surrounding if bug bounties can replace traditional pentests, in my opinion I wouldn't say they can replace them however in some cases can go hand in hand with them.

A bug bounty platform/program is more suited to the external network and perimeter than it is to an internal network however this reality might change in the coming years, who am I to predict the future!

Penetration Testing

The vast majority of folks reading this book, your aspirations will be to land a job for a consultancy as a pentester. Do you know what it takes to learn the art and what is required though? So far in this book I've covered off the basic technical and general skillsets that are required, however what is day to day like for a pentester?

Generally speaking, as a penetration tester (have a giggle, go on it is a funny title) will vary depending on who you are working for, what region you're working in and what area your team covers. Taking the UK as an example (where I'm from), most testers will be widely skilled in many areas in the field with a core knowledge base in web application testing & infrastructure testing.

However, this base isn't the only type of testing or work that a tester will undertake, typically this will also encompass wireless testing, configuration reviews, thick client reviews, phishing, social engineering & some other more bespoke areas such as hardware hacking & embedded system breakouts.

In a way you could call the UK market pretty mature when it comes to testers based upon the skillsets held by a vast majority, note that these skillsets will be gained overtime and that you likely won't be expected to know about them all from the off so don't worry if you're a junior starting out.

By contrast testers in the US tend to be focused more on one area or another with very few delivering the vast degree of services. This isn't a call out of US testers it is purely an observation that many consultancies will choose one area and focus on it.

Meaning, their consultants will only deliver web application testing(appsec) or infrastructure(netsec) or red teaming or something else and specialise in this area, there's no doubt that some will be able to deliver the others mentioned above but the specialism will mean a high percentage of deliverable work will lie in the area of specialism.

All testers will share one common denominator which is reporting. Some people love it, many hate it, I personally thoroughly enjoy it. Alongside the hacking, the main product that your client is paying for is the report as it is the final deliverable.

Bug Bounty Hunting

Now the other legal route for someone learning about penetration testing techniques and hacking will be bug bounties. Like penetration testing bug bounties have a similar area of skillsets whereby an individual can pick their targets and choose what skills to hone in.

My personal view on it (and this is my opinion) is that for many it is a full time job but I feel it is not as sustainable as a career doing pentesting, sure you'll probably earn more in the short term however doing pentesting in most situations will get you a salary in which you'll get paid at the end of the month regardless.

It is however a fantastic opportunity to do and even if you work as a pentester by day, partaking in bug bounties in your evenings will serve you well as it exposes you to different systems, techniques and generally (unless you're red teaming all the time) more open scopes.

They allow you to home in on areas in which you have the most interest and try to perfect different techniques whilst still being able to report back your findings to the specific vendors. If you're interested in getting involved there are several platforms out there:

- Synack[170]
- Hackerone[171]
- BugCrowd[172]

All of which have different ways of doing things, different programs and different researchers. I'd highly recommend you check them out and give them some time to get a feel for it. Who knows maybe you'll make your millions and learn loads whilst doing it!

The bottom line being that both have their pros and cons however what you choose to do is your decision, if you can though give both a chance for sure!

Coloured Teams

Red Team, Blue Team, Purple Team, Black Team... Rainbow team? What are all of these things and what do they all mean? Is this a new case of a new found buzzword bingo or do they have a place and a purpose?

The coloured teams are something that is thrown around a lot and while some of them are better known than others I hope

---
[170] https://www.synack.com
[171] https://www.hackerone.com
[172] https://bugcrowd.com

to break them down in this post and make it all a little clearer for you, the reader.

So, rewind a second, what are the different types of teaming, why do they exist and what is their purpose. While some are used and chatted about a lot in the industry others are rarely used, the list below details each colour and the primary role of said team: - Red Team – Attackers, simulating adversaries and conducting offensive security, the red team's goal is to simulate threats against an organisation and effectively test the security measures implemented by an organisation. - Blue Team – Defenders, keeping the network and users secure :-), they have the hardest job arguably. Their job is to protect and defend an organisation's assets from threats and act on detections. - Purple Team – Act as a mediator between red and blue they are tasked with boosting the effectiveness of the Red and Blue teams. The purple team add value with insight from attackers but with added incident response and defensive practices to effectively up skill both sides and improve security over all. - Yellow Team – The general builders, usually software dev or architects responsible for creation of networks, software or implementation of other assets. - Green Team – Builders who change their design and implementation based on defense knowledge, similar to the orange team however instead of taking cues from the red team, these are drawn from defensive practices. - Orange Team -Building based on input from attacker knowledge, the orange team is made up of a yellow team but with direct input from a red team mindset, which results in adaptations of implementations based on attacker knowledge. - Black Team – Usually referred to as physical security assessments, the naming is drawn from black op engagements whereby the teams used to dress in all black to carry out stealth operations.

Follow me on Twitter https://twitter.com/ZephrFish

Key features of a black op(eration) are that it is secret and it is not attributable to the organisation carrying it out. - White Team – The team that establishes the rules of engagement and are usually the employees of the organisation who are undertaking a red or purple team engagement. The white team does not conduct any testing.

Given the overview detailed above I'm going to deep dive into three of the many teams in this post; Red, Blue and Purple. Anyone working in attack-defend areas of security will have likely heard of blue being defensive and red being offensive security, some may have even heard of purple as being a mix of the two. I've pulled together this section to try and smash through the nonsense being thrown about describing and selling each as a different thing.

TL;DR The red team attacks and the blue team defends. The purple team mediates between the two offering insight from both a blue and red perspective.

Red Team

A red team engagement is an objective-based assessment that requires a holistic view of the organisation from the perspective of an adversary. This assessment process is designed to meet the needs of complex organisations handling a variety of sensitive assets through technical, physical, or process-based means.

The purpose of carrying out a red team assessment is to demonstrate how real world attackers can combine exploits and tactics to achieve their goal. It is an effective way to show that even the most sophisticated technology in the world means very little if an attacker can walk out of the data centre with an un-encrypted hard drive. Instead of relying on a single network appliance to secure sensitive data, it's better to take a defense in depth approach and continuously improve your people, process, and technology.

Red Teams are brought in by mature organisations to assess their blue team to ensure that, should a real world attack occur, the defensive capabilities are sufficiently tested and prepared.

Blue Team

The blue team are the good folks that often do not get enough praise, they are the real heroes in this story. The blue team are the front line defenders who work at all levels to protect a network from nefarious activity and help to secure businesses day in day out. Their primary role is to act as the varying lines of defense of companies' networks, similar to the offensive side of security blue teamers come in many flavours.

While I have never worked in blue team roles, I do have a lot of friends who work in the sphere, so my knowledge is second hand from speaking to them and reading for myself. I have however implemented defensive practices in lab environments and written about them before but I am by no means an expert on the subject.

Purple Team

The point with purple-teams being, the collaboration and clear goals of security improvement, education and attacker insight for internal security teams. They do this by integrating the defensive tactics and controls from the blue team with the threats and vulnerabilities found by the red team into a single narrative that maximizes both. Ideally purple shouldn't be a team at all, but rather a permanent dynamic between red and blue. Although they share a common goal, red and blue teams are often not aligned or informed with open communications, which leads to businesses not leveraging the full value of their combined teams' expertise. Red teams and blue teams should be encouraged to work as a collaborative team, to share insights beyond reporting, with a primary focus on creation of a strong feedback loop to create a more diverse security model, and to look for detection and prevention controls that can realistically be implemented for immediate improvement. The beauty of purple teams is that both sides give insight into similar problems with a different perspective thus collaboration can create effective solutions to complex problems.

The Importance of Purple, Red and Blue

While red teaming is lots of fun, I've found a new love for bypassing defensive measures then helping folks improve. One could argue the point in a red team is to assess an organisation's ability to detect and triage a real threat. Part of this is assessing the blue team's capability as to how different processes kick in to triage and irradiate threats/risks on the network however often this varies depending on the organisation and the maturity of the defensive teams.

There are a few reasons people undertake security testing, the majority of reasons either come down to a requirement from 3rd parties or compliance. However sometimes for a company to take security seriously they need to have been breached or suffered an attack of some sort, and at this point pen testing can be too late. Thus implementing a robust security arm of the business is key.

Red, blue and purple teaming are the way in which an organisation should be addressing their security implementations across the business. If you as a business are relying on an annual pen test and traditional anti-virus to protect your business against threats then it's already game over. If you've done simulated attacks in the past where the measurement of success is if red bypasses x or blue spots y but the engagement is taken no further, then who is learning or gaining value from this?

11. Hacking Your Career Path

Having the technical skills are great, going to meet-ups and making the social contacts is even better. What really gets you in the door though? Knowing people? A CV? Being somewhat known? All valid points and questions, all worth looking into and all will get you somewhere.

Things to Consider

The main thing that I hear again and again is to get a job you need to sell yourself to an employer. What do you do or have that Joe/Jane Doe does not? The few main things I would recommend that you do are:

- 1) Create a blog[173]
- 2) Keep it up to date with projects you're doing, write-ups & tutorials(all optional of course, however will stand you in good stead).
- 3) Go along to conferences and actually speak to people, if you're new to the industry make up business cards with your blog and email on them, hand them to folks who you make contact with. Who knows you may call upon them at a later stage, it might not be this month or this years but say three or four years down the line they

---
[173]https://blog.zsec.uk/about

might be the hiring manager in a new position you are applying for?

On the note of conferences, try and submit talks, get yourself out there and try to get a point across be it learning a particular area in the industry that you're really enjoying and want others to hear about too or another area that has peaked your interest. Take it by the horns and go for it, submit to Call For Participation/Papers (CFPs), most conferences will have a rookie or noob track, give it a go. You'll be surprised at how many folks will come along and support you.

By creating a blog you are doing two things essentially, you're creating a log of the projects you do outside of your studies or in your spare time and what you're also doing is demonstrating your ability to write things down.

Advertising Skillset

Typically the first engagement you'll have with a potential employer is either face to face at an event or by sending your CV out to them. If it is the first my advice would be, just be careful what you say to people and how you approach different situations however that's just general life advice! Keep in mind that that one individual you see today may well end up being your employer or employee tomorrow.

When it comes to CVs though, the best thing you can do is write it yourself, especially if you're applying for a role in infosec that involves reporting. As a full disclosure I'm not a careers expert however I have seen many CVs in my time in the industry.

Follow me on Twitter https://twitter.com/ZephrFish

Selling Yourself

Getting that disclaimer out of the way, taking penetration testing as an example job you're applying for. You want to craft your CV in a way that it peaks the reader's attention from opening it (`CV_totes_not_malware.pdf.exe` <- don't do this).

Typically the core details you'll want to include should include; a blurb about yourself, employment/education history, hobbies/achievements + any professional certifications you've gained(this is things like OSCP & GPEN etc) however if you don't have these fair not, it's not the end of the world.

Your Introduction

When writing your CV you need to be mindful of your target audience. This can depend on where you're applying for i.e. are you applying to a massive corporation who will likely filter based on certifications or are you applying to a small outfit who are more likely to read your CV despite certs?

Either way you want to hit the ground running with a one to two page highlight of how awesome you are and why you're the person they need! In your introduction blurb you want to tailor this to the audience, so for a corporation you might want to start out by explaining you have x, y & z certifications and are active in x community or have done y as a profession for z years etc. An example blurb may look similar to:

> Andy has worked in information security for just under 10 years combined, focussed specifically on penetration testing, having achieved >OSCP & Crest

> Registered Tester (CRT), He is a CHECK Team member (CTM) and has delivered several CHECK tests. Andy is currently working >towards Crest Certified Tester(CCT-Inf) and CHECK Team Leader (CTL) status. Alongside his work in pentesting, he also spends his free >time doing bug bounties and has identified many bugs in several companies.

This is written in the third person however you can write in first person too, this is mainly down to personal preference. The blurb above covers off my experience, qualifications, aspirations & involvement with bug bounties. Your mileage will likely vary as you might not have experience within industry, just starting out you have more to play with when it comes to this intro text. An extended intro that I have used in the past looks similar to this:

> I am an old school hacker in the sense that I like to take things apart and look at their inner workings them. My background has always >been computer related, I currently work as a Penetration Tester and as a researcher in my free time. I hold a Bachelor of Engineering in >Digital Security Forensics and Ethical Hacking. Previously I worked as a computer technician, working with both software and hardware on >a variety of platforms, such as OSX, Windows and Linux.
>
> I participate in karate three times a week and currently hold a 1st Dan black belt; I have fought at Full contact level and in mixed >martial arts competitions. I like to apply the same mind set to pentesting as I do with karate, which usually

---

Follow me on Twitter https://twitter.com/ZephrFish

involves hard work and some >pain the next day, if you are not exhausted at the end and feeling accomplished, you are doing it wrong.

This is different to the first block of text as it only includes two achievements that I held at that stage, these being a degree & my black belt in Karate. However what it does include is a description of me as a person with some highlights of things I have experience working with.

The bottom line being, your intro is what an employer is going to see first, so **make yourself stand out**.

Laying Things Out

As I've said previously, I'm not a careers or CV expert however I've found the following layout to work. Note that this will vary depending on what you are applying for though.

If your employment history is lacking or you've not worked in industry at all before something like the following might work for you:

- Achievements & Hobbies
- Skillset
- Employment
- Education

This can be switched up depending on what sits nicer or if you have more of one thing you want your potential employer to see first put this above the others.

Achievements & Hobbies

In your achievements and hobbies maybe include research you've done or capture the flag events you've taken part in. Some examples to include might include blog write-ups, projects you've contributed to on Github or similar, if you're involved in Bug Bounties - include where you've been featured in halls of fame. Try including other achievements outside of technology that might be interesting, maybe you're active in sports/fitness and have won something. Or you help out with a community project. Examples I could include would be:

- Write a blog that is read by 50,000 readers a month (https://blog.zsec.uk)
- Organiser of Defcon Glasgow (DC44141)
- Active in Bug Bounties
    - Hall of Fame: Adobe, Starbucks, Mindgeek, Worldpay, Homebrew, Oracle, Facebook
    - Found ~120 Bugs total in many different companies
- Hold 1st Dan Blackbelt in Karate
    - Training for 14 years
    - Have taught both Kids and Adults
    - Competed at full contact level
- Spoken at Hack In The Box Amsterdam 2015, various technical talks available https://blog.zsec.uk/about
- Holds Enhanced Disclosure from Disclosure Scotland (PVG)

As can be seen an inclusion of a mix of both technical and social/sporting achievements can help. However don't worry if you are lacking in the achievements area, spin up a blog and start writing, try some capture the flag events in your spare time. Then add these in later.

Follow me on Twitter https://twitter.com/ZephrFish

Skillset

In the skillset section, try to include what areas of technologies you feel you are good at. So if you prefer mobile applications note this down, include what else you're comfortable with, so if you've done OSCP you might put down that you can do infrastructure testing to a degree. If you do a lot of bug bounties with web apps, you could include that, something like:

- Web Application Penetration Testing
- Open-Source Intelligence Gathering
- Public Speaking
- Mobile Application Testing Experience
- Worked with Windows, *Unix & MacOS
    - Able to build review Windows, Unix & MacOS
- Experience with Wireless Testing
- Competent with Hardware hacking & soldering

The main thing to keep in mind is being **honest** about your skillset. If your CV gets you an interview an employer is well within their right to ask you about your skillset or anything mentioned in your CV.

If you put down you know about hardware hacking then the interviewer asks you to describe the different logic levels you might come across when dealing with an embedded device and you sit blank expression it will be apparent you might have told a wee lie on that ol' CV of yours. You don't really want to be in this situation if you can help it.

Employment & Education

Another common thing I have seen with CVs in the past is people listing their entire employment history since the beginning of time meaning their CV is a million pages in length. If you've worked in lots of different jobs or had minor part time jobs try to only note the relevant ones on your CV, or alternatively note them all down but only include a paragraph about the ones that are relevant:

- ACME IT Support: **Senior Technician** 2015-2017
    - Dealt with hardware and software
    - Customer service experience
    - Phone and onsite support
- ACME Bank: **Security Intern** May 2012 - September 2012
    - Logging Phishing Attempts
    - Developed Automation of Logging
    - Worked with CERT

Note above that the key skills used in the relevant positions have been included rather than padding out the section massively; remember your CV should ideally fit on one page, either double or single sided. The same goes with education history, depending on your stage in life/age/education try to be concise about it with relevant certifications put first.

- Offensive Security Wireless Professional (OSWP): March 2017
- Offensive Security Certified Professional (OSCP): Feb 2017
- Glasgow University: BSc Computer Science 2010 - 2014
- High School Example: 5 Highers including Computing & Maths 2004 - 2010

Creating a Blog

Now at this stage you might be reading this thinking, that advice is great, but I don't have a blog or maybe you do but you don't have any ideas as to what to include on your blog?

If you fall into the first group and you don't have a blog, you can spin one up fairly easily there are lots of options out there things like medium & GitHub offer free options to create a blog and start writing or if you're happy to spend a wee bit of money Digital Ocean[174] have instance of ghost which you can deploy from $5/Month which is what this blog runs.

Once you have a blog setup get some things written up, try some capture the flags and do some write ups or maybe you've found a cool bug on a bug bounty try writing it up in a blog post(if the company agree that you can disclose it). If you haven't done any CTFs try some of the exercises from vulnhub[175] or pentester lab[176] and write up your solution. Alternatively maybe you've started learning an area and want to share your experience try doing that too!

Or even better, maybe you've learned about something new and want to write a tutorial like this one, shove that up on your blog then tweet it out or share on social media to drive traffic.

When you've got your blog all setup with some content try to include it on your CV or share with the community to help others(this will stand you in good stead in the future). The other benefit of a blog is it begins a pipeline of work you've done which you can show to future employers or potentially clients.

---
[174]https://m.do.co/c/24ca2070f1f5
[175]https://www.vulnhub.com
[176]https://www.pentesterlab.com

Overall good luck with whatever you decide to do, remember a few key things though:

- Always be clear
- Be Honest
- Show your interesting side!

12. Further Reading & Resources

Books to Read

There are literally hundreds of different books for all aspects of security, the sections below list only a select few that I've either read or have been recommended in the past to check out.

Network Pentesting

Having read all of these I can recommend them all, each serving a different purpose but overall covering off network pentesting topics.

- Network Security Assessment: Know Your Network [177] - Chris Mcnabb has produced 2 editions before this one and this serves as an update to the 2nd edition bringing together different techniques for network enumeration and fingerprinting.
- The Hacker Playbook 2 [178] & - The Hacker Playbook 3 [179] - A practical guide which follows a similar methodology to the Infrastructure section of this book.

---

[177] http://amzn.to/2rcHrum
[178] http://amzn.to/2pK30kR
[179] https://amzn.to/2Cx6r7H

- Penetration Testing: A Hands on guide to hacking[180] - This lends its hand to the hacker playbook 2 however gives a deeper overview of the different aspects within penetration testing.

Programming

Below are some books to check out in relation to learning programming.

- Learn Python The Hardway[181] - A good introduction to python for any level, Zed A Shaw takes you through lots of exercises to teach the basics.
- Learn C The Hardway[182] - The same as Learn Python the hardway but for C.
- Learn Ruby The Hardway[183] - - The same as Learn Python the hardway but for Ruby.
- Violent Python[184] - A more hands on guide to writing python code for penetration testing & offensive security.

Web Application Testing

Here are the core essentials to get you started after reading this book, if you want to dive deeper into web apps these four links will set you right.

---

[180] http://amzn.to/2pJPi1C
[181] http://amzn.to/2qh6EEP
[182] http://amzn.to/2pK16km
[183] http://amzn.to/2pJZAPj
[184] http://amzn.to/2qE1fuu

- Web Hacking 101[185] by yaworsk[186] - I highly recommend checking Pete's book out, it has a collection of bug bounty reports and resources for information on different findings others in the field have found and disclosed to companies.
- Web Application Hackers Handbook 2[187] - This is a bit dated in terms of reading material however the underlying fundamentals are still applicable to testing now a days. The physical books are nice to have however you can source them on the internet using advanced Google searches, but I'll leave that up to you.
- Mastering Modern Web Applications[188] - A newer take on web application penetration testing, it has some great resources and information contained within it. Stacks up well alongside WAHH2.
- Hacking with Github[189] - A repository of writeups, guides and information on web application hacking and testing. Well worth spending some time reading up on the resources available to better your skillset and knowledge regardless of your level every day is a school day and you should always be willing to look into new things learn a new skill or technique everyday.

Quick Reference for Bag

All of these guides are really useful for when you're onsite with no access to the Internet.

[185] https://leanpub.com/web-hacking-101
[186] https://twitter.com/yaworsk
[187] http://amzn.to/1NOwTvt
[188] http://amzn.to/2gnfRqb
[189] https://github.com/infoslack/awesome-web-hacking

- Bash Pocket Reference[190]
- PowerShell Pocket Reference[191]
- Red Team Field Manual[192]
- Blue Team Field Manual[193]
- Purple Team Field Manual[194]
- Operator Handbook[195] - this is a little on the heavy side but it does provide a lot of information around how to do different activities in red and blue teaming.

Web Applications for Learning on

- Damn Vulnerable Web Application(DVWA)[196]
- OWASP Web Goat[197]
- OWASP List of Vulnerable Web Applications[198]
- PentesterLab - A Collection of Exercises to Learn Testing[199]
- VulnHub - Not specifically all web app learning but some great VMs to play with[200]
- CTFTime[201] - Not exactly web applications, however capture the flag events can be a great way to grow your skillsets
- Over The Wire[202]
- Hack The Box[203] - This requires a bit of a challenge to

---

[190] http://amzn.to/2rdNUq0
[191] http://amzn.to/2pJODxe
[192] http://amzn.to/2qh7WzF
[193] http://amzn.to/2rdEyKB
[194] https://amzn.to/3qiihtj
[195] https://amzn.to/2Oh4cef
[196] http://www.dvwa.co.uk/
[197] https://www.owasp.org/index.php/WebGoat_Installation
[198] https://www.owasp.org/index.php/OWASP_Vulnerable_Web_Applications_Directory_Project/Pages/Offline
[199] https://pentesterlab.com/
[200] https://www.offensive-security.com/labs/
[201] https://ctftime.org
[202] http://overthewire.org/wargames/
[203] https://hackthebox.eu

Follow me on Twitter https://twitter.com/ZephrFish

sign up but there's lots of free challenges once you're in! *hint* there's no invite code ;)
- TryHackMe[204] - Similar to hackthebox but has a more entry level approach and enables you to learn different topics in rooms.

People to Follow on Twitter

I am a massive believer in passing knowlege on always and the list of individuals below have shared some great knowledge with me and the community. I'd actively encourage you to give them a follow to learn more.

- Sean[205] - A bug hunter who produces some great tutorials for the community and who has a vast degree of knowledge in web application testing.
- Paul Ritchie[206] - My mentor who got me into the industry and gave me the leg up, he tweets about web and other interesting things.
- Paul[207] - One of the most motivated individuals I've ever met in my life who went from working in system adminstration to becoming a pentester in under a year! He has written some great articles about getting into the field and different ways of looking at things.
- Adam[208] - A red teamer by trade with some fantastic pwnage skills, Adam does great writeups on reverse engineering & pwning general stuffs. A great dude who produces a great blog.

---

[204] https://tryhackme.com/
[205] https://twitter.com/zseano
[206] https://twitter.com/cornerpirate
[207] https://twitter.com/infosecps
[208] https://twitter.com/_xpn_

12. Further Reading & Resources

- Dan Card[209] - A builder come breaker who is always posting threads of labs he is building, he builds a lot of capture the flag challenges and has a wealth of experience.
- Me[210] - I tend to retweet posts and content around offensive security and some blue team stuff too, I also post about new blog posts and cars ;).

There are many many more folks to follow on twitter surrounding a variety of topics but mainly the few above I've learned a tonne from and would recommend you check them out.

Links to Checkout

Alongside books and twitter here are some blogs and other sites you should check out to learn more about the security industry & different kinds of writeups.

- CornerPirate's Blog[211] - Another Paul! This time with great tips on the other bits of testing like reporting and creating things.
- Cyber Security Challenge UK[212] - A great resouce for those of you in the UK, CSC run events all over the country that help aid those interested in getting into the field.
- Tulpas OSCP Prep Guide[213] - A well orchestrated prep guide for OSCP.

---

[209]https://twitter.com/UK_Daniel_Card
[210]https://twitter.com/ZephrFish
[211]https://cornerpirate.com
[212]https://cybersecuritychallenge.org.uk
[213]https://tulpasecurity.files.wordpress.com/2016/09/tulpa-pwk-prep-guide1.pdf

---

Follow me on Twitter https://twitter.com/ZephrFish

- zseano's Blog[214] - Sean's blog takes you through some great web appliation penetration testing tutorials.
- Reddit Netsec Thread[215] - Latest news in information security on reddit.
- Portswigger's Blog[216] - Information on the latest exploit techniques for web applications, brought to you by the creators of Burp suite.
- TJ Null's OSCP Guide[217]

Thank You

Thank you for buying or downl0ading(if you've pulled a copy when it's been free on my publisher or pirated it!) this book, I hope you've learned at least one thing from reading it. Please feel free to message me on twitter[218] or email me[219] some feedback and your thoughts on the book.

As this is an ebook(or physical if you are one of the lucky ones!) I plan to keep adding to it as feedback comes in, expanding some sections & correcting others; you will be emailed if there is a significant change made or new area added. Now you've read this, all that is left is to say best of luck in the industry, I hope you continue to develop and learn. If you see me at a conference please come and say hello, I'm always happy to speak to folks! Who knows maybe this might inspire you to write your own book, if you do please let me know!

---

[214] http://zseano.com
[215] https://www.reddit.com/r/netsec
[216] http://blog.portswigger.net
[217] https://www.netsecfocus.com/oscp/2021/05/06/The_Journey_to_Try_Harder-_TJnull-s_Preparation_Guide_for_PEN-200_PWK_OSCP_2.0.html
[218] https://www.twitter.com/ZephrFish
[219] mailto:book@pornhub.ninja

Follow me on Twitter https://twitter.com/ZephrFish

For those reading in 2021, I am in the process of #LTR102 and hope to publish it in 2022, so stay tuned! You can sign up to be notified when it is released here[220].

---

[220] https://leanpub.com/LTR102-Expanding-Your-Security-Horizons

---

Follow me on Twitter https://twitter.com/ZephrFish

Made in the USA
Monee, IL
03 March 2024